Team Building: A Guide For The Reluctant Manager

By

Lawrence G Fine

Team Building: A guide for the reluctant
manager
Copyright © 2009 by (Kick It, LLC)

Table of Contents

Introduction

How many of us really want to have the responsibility of leadership? Many people say they want to be the boss, but the truth is the majority of us are reluctant or unwilling to take on leadership responsibilities.

How many times have you been sent on a course? Did you learn all the different ways manage or supervise staff? It was wonderful in the classroom setting, where your peers were people learning the same skills. You might have done some role playing during you time on the course, which again might have been fairly easy to master. However, did you discover how it was completely different when you had to put all your training into practice and become the manager or supervisor of staff at your company?

You know it doesn't take long to realize people

are very different. Now this isn't some big revelation but it is true, but you will find some people are difficult regardless of the situation or circumstances, whereas, others who were easy going can suddenly become difficult to manage.

Yet, there are other problems when you move from being a team member to managing the team. You'll find some people who were excellent team members when you were part of the team. But, these same people will react and interact in a totally differently way to you when you become their team leader, or manager.

Suddenly, the team dynamics become more difficult, especially if one of the team members considers they would make a better team leader or manager than you. Watch quietly, how is the person now behaving compared to your appointment as their manager? Didn't it change? Could the reason being they are jealous of your success, and they are trying to do everything possible to make you fail?

This is one of the main reasons why making the step to manage people who were once team members with you, on working on the same level is difficult. People know what is going to happen, and it has become a daunting prospect.

What job title do you have and is it important? The answer is simple. The job title you have or are given is unimportant. What is your title? You might be an officer in the Marines; Army; Navy; or Air Force. You might manage a business or sports team. You might be a team leader; director; CEO; CIO; or even a business owner. You can add many other job titles to the list, and as you see the list of job titles can be endless. Yet, in the final analysis the job title doesn't matter. Why? Because the managing of a team will require at least some effort by you and it will take a lot of your time. If you are not prepared to do the work required for your position in the company you work for or the team you oversee, then you will fail.

We will use the term **manager** through the book to refer to someone's line manager; project leader; or direct supervisor.

We have taken examples from many different sources throughout this book. The main illustrations have come from soccer, but we will draw on the Bible; literature; history; films; and personal experience. These will help us to start to understand some of the problems we may face as we manage people. The good news is we shouldn't expect to face all the problems, but by reading and understanding, we start in a position of strength as we manage our team.

Over and over again we are reminded of whom we are dealing with; it is people. We need to remember they are not slaves, or commodities, but people, fellow human beings.

We will always get different reactions to the things we do or say, and you will find some people will react well to you, but other people will react badly to anything you say and do. This is human nature, and if someone decides to take a dislike to you, then you will always be working from a negative position in their thinking, and you will have to try and knock down the wall they have built up in their minds, before they will accept you and the role you are in.

You can spend many days or even months trying to analyze what changed, but the simple answer often is the roles changed, and they are unable to accept it. However, you might also find other factors are causing the problems. It might not be your fault; you might remind them of a negative experience they once faced. It might be their upbringing means they have problems with people of different races; color of skin; religion or creed.

However, there is no substitute for managing yourself on a day-to-day; month-by-month and year-by-year basis. When you manage a team, you need to remember you are also a team member and the managing starts with you.

You will also find there is always more to do – you will never finally complete the team. How do we mean, especially when you know your team is going to be a set number of people? A team isn't complete just because the right number of people is on it. You will find when everything looks good, with no conflicts within the team, and the work can be completed, something will change. This is why your team will never be completed.

It may look like a curved ball in baseball, a bouncer in cricket, but the result is more work to be done in less time and maybe with fewer staff. You'll also find problems and troubles come in all shapes and sizes but it will come. If you're expecting it, you can be prepared for it in advanced. You might not know what the problems will be, but being prepared for something to happen, so you can deal with it quickly an effectively. Is saying you will have problems and troubles being negative? No! It is being realistic. Don't bury your head in the sand, and hope the will disappear overnight. Deal with them headfirst, and get them out of the way.

We will find situations will change, and work very rarely diminishes.

A senior manager was told to go and close down all the car dealerships he managed in a country in the Far East. He worked methodically through each once, and closed them all down, ensuring all the paperwork was completed and correct.

He returned to his office with the knowledge, because he had closed down all the dealerships and fired all of his staff, it would be probable; he would be the one who lost his job next. Yes, this worked exactly as he expected, and he was laid off from his job.

If you have ever wondered what could be the worse thing you have to do as a manager this is it. It is the knowledge, the work the team members are currently doing is a dead end task and the team will be disbanded with all team members losing their jobs. Yet, it is your job as the manager to keep them motivated even though the rumors are flying, people are saying jobs are being lost, or companies are being closed. This is even worse during a recession.

Who is the reluctant manager? It is anyone who is a reluctant team leader. You may not fall into the role yet, but most of us feel some reluctance to lead other people.

The method behind the chapters is to dip in to one chapter to see what you are doing and how it fits into various real-life situations. You may have become a team leader after a disaster; you should read the chapter on disasters, which will enable you to keep a perspective on the job you have been given to complete.

Chapter 1 Understand Where You Fit Into The Whole

It was a great day; you've been offered a new job or promotion and have decided to accept it. As you think about it, you realize you now have to start in a position where you are part of a team, but you are also the team leader in another team. This might be a difficult time, especially if you are working at your old job, before starting your new job.

Before you start the new post you'll need to understand where you and your team fit into the organization.

In business you might be part of a small company which has one site then you think it will be relatively easy, yet some small companies don't have a structure in place for their teams. For multi-national companies with many locations set up in USA, Europe, Australasia and the Far East it becomes more difficult. You only have to look at companies such as Hewlett-Packard (HP), Glaxo and Air Product to realize all companies are not equal in terms of their organization. It might be possible to locate your team in an internal department and know how the department relates to the whole. Allowing for the complexity of the size of organization, we need to look at the team we are leading and where the team fits into the whole organization.

When it comes to sports, someone may argue with soccer you only have the team you are leading or managing, and this will make it an easier job. However, when you consider the many clubs which have a history you don't only have the one main team.

Let's look at some of the famous soccer teams in the United Kingdom, clubs like Manchester

United; Liverpool; and Arsenal; just to name a few. What are the teams they have; you always have your first team and a reserve team without looking any further. But when you look further, you'll find they have a number of junior teams who will also be playing and needing leadership.

Today, we find there are more and more ladies teams in the field of soccer. As an example, you'll find Arsenal has a ladies team, which is one of the most successful around.

When you look at the wider club, you will see there will be people whose job it is to maintain the training grounds, and the main pitches. The teams don't want to turn up to play a game on a ground which hasn't been maintained and has broken pieces of glass or pottery, and grass which is a few inches tall.

Another important job within the club is the

people who specialize in merchandising and ticketing (both match by match and season tickets).

Every aspect of a game is a team effort, and it is the manager's job to hold all levels together and organize his or her team. It is important for the first team manager to be aware of the other teams within the club, in terms of playing and logistical help. The first team manager also needs to know who from the current team members are going to be available next season, and look at which ones should play for the first team. Finally, a soccer club will have different levels of team leaders or managers, yet it is important for each person to not only know but understands where they fit into the whole club.

Understand The Organizations Aims

Do you understand the organization or

company's aims? You will find a company can have many levels; and you should be able to view the aims of your organization. You might find these summarized in the Tag line, which you see on all their advertising. For other businesses, you will have to concentrate on the aims and purpose statements circulated within the company. Regardless, of how the company shares their aims, you need to find out what they are, and also to try and understand them. If you find it to difficult to do, then ask, people should then be able to explain it simply to you.

Tag Line

Every business needs a tag line, but the biggest problem is coming up with something short and memorable. Let's be real here, not every business can afford to hire a top company who will work on this for you, because you are paying them top dollars to come up with the perfect tag line. Yet, within your business you might find team members who will be able to do exactly this, there will be the creative people who are willing to use their skills to create the perfect tag line for the company.

If you can't find the one person you're looking for, then why not make it a team event? Gather the team together, and ask every member brainstorm and give ideas. Let them know you are looking for ideas, and their idea might be the one used by the company. Also, let those team members know how every one of them is important, and you want to have their ideas and feedback.

How important are tag line? Do you know how many you can name without thinking? This is why they are important. Think for a short moment and try and find some of the really memorable tag lines for companies?

Airline companies have been using tag lines for a long time.

British Airways "The World's Favourite Airline" is the one most of us remember, but the new one they are currently using is "The Way To Fly."

Lufthansa with their "There's No Better Way To Fly."
America Airlines is "Something Special in the Air."

Cathay Pacific on the other hand seems to change it's tag line every time it gets a new advertising campaign with slogans like "Now You're Really Flying It's Better Than The Old One," "Try Before You Fly," and "Now You're Really Flying."

Many sports companies have very simple but memorable tag lines.

"Just Do It" is from Nike. How many times has this been quoted not only in the sports field, but as a motivational quote, to get people to "take action?"

"Impossible Is Nothing" from Adidas seems to not only say something about the brand, but what they expect from those who are supported when wearing their sportswear.

We also have medical companies; again they have their tag lines, because they are important.

Glaxo has "On The brink Of Discovery," and this concentrates on their role to discover new medicines for their customers. But, you will find this is in contrasts with the newer corporate tag line for GlaxoSmithKline "Do More, Feel Better, and Live Longer."

Air Products and Chemicals ask people to "Tell Me More."

British Oxygen promotes, they are "More Than Just Gas..."

When it comes to soccer some teams having a tag line, you will find some who have taken them from a song which then becomes their anthem.

Liverpool, you will see on their team badge "You'll never walk alone."

There is so much which could be said about tag lines, because so many companies have one. You will find large corporations spend millions of US$ to get just the right tag line. Some use the same tag line for years, but others will use it for one sales promotion and then throw it away, until the next promotion when they have to find another one to use.

Being a part of a large corporation it is essential for you know and understand the tag line. You do not simply need to say it parrot fashion at meetings and conferences, but you should really understand where this places you in terms of the industry you belong to and the customers you serve.

The customer can be the one who makes or breaks your business. One disgruntled customer can do enormous damage as they complain to their friends; family and enemies. Yet, on the other hand a good customer might not say anything about you, they know you are beneficial to their business, and they don't want to give this information to their competitors, because they know they have the advantages from all you and your company offers. Business is sometimes a strange place to work in.

Mission Statement

A great tag line is the beginning, but you must have a mission statement to go with it. Whereas, the tag lines goes wherever a product or service from a company is advertised or promoted, Mission statements are more for the internal company use.

A Mission Statement aim is to provide focus and motivation to the employees in their everyday job. This motivation must be for every level of employee within the company. This will mean it has to be understandable for those with highly technical and technological jobs, together with those who manage and direct the company, down to those whose jobs are the most mundane. Why should it be for all the people? Because everybody regardless of the job they do, is important to the company. There is always a place in the large organizations for those who are prepared to do the mundane tasks well. It doesn't matter if it is the processing of orders, the ordering of spare parts or supplies to the accounting of the payments which come in. There is very little glamour about these tasks but they are essential to keep the company functioning.

As a manager you'll need to understand the mission statement and see how it relates to what you and your team do on a regular basis. For example, British Airways wouldn't be "The World's Favorite Airline" for very long if the cleaners didn't clean the planes, and the mechanics didn't maintain them well.

Safety and hygiene are two important aspects of any company, and yet one which is either taken for granted, or ignored by the management when they praise the effort of the team.

Understand How The Department Fits Into The Organization

Have you tried to see where you fit into your organization? It isn't easy, especially as there is so much linking within the company. It makes it easier to understand if you can see a high-level organization chart for the organization which you are part of. Where do you fit into your organization's chart? You might need to talk and confirm with your boss, and this might also be a good time to confirm the goals for your team.

What you should remember is at times when a CEO (or other business owner) started with the organization they might have started at the bottom of the organization; and they often will get promoted within the department they were first employed in.

When it's time for the CEO to leave their

department, he tends to take the ideas and ways things were done in the department with him, and it can lead to some bizarre organizational charts, and even more bizarre lines of reporting. You'll find sometimes the way department's link together in the company, are of a historical nature rather than being a deliberate design. One of the common linking of department is the computer department being linked either directly or indirectly with the accounting department. This is because the accounting department was the first department to be computerized within the organization.

By understanding where you fit in the organization, you will begin to understand the pressures you are under from your line management to complete some of the tasks which you and your team are responsible for. You will also see where there are tasks which relate to other departments and why relating to them is also important. A team member does not need this awareness but the manager does, because it allows the work to flow freely through the team and out to others.

You will find for a soccer first team manager, this isn't so much a problem. The manager will relate directly with the board of directors, who will give the direction the club needs to take in the current season and the finances which will be available from the board.

When it comes to budgeting and managing the books this is something every manager needs to understand and do. It is important for every team manager needs to be aware of their budget. The complexity comes with all the other teams within the club. How do they all relate to the first team and the first team reserves?

Does the under-18 team have a role to supply its best players to the reserves or even the first team should disaster strike? You might think it would be hard for the complete 22-strong first team to be out of action. This is true, but given a long enough period of time, disasters do happen. We will see later the effects of an air crash on one soccer club. Today we are facing a pandemic influenza, but even in a bad winter an entire team could go down with influenza. Where are your other team members when there is a game for your first team and you don't have eleven players fit from the first team squad? This is where the whole club comes into its own. We must be flexible to meet the competitive needs of the whole club.

Understand The Role Of Your Team

Have you consider a soccer team? Do you think the role of the manager is to ensure his team wins all of its games and finishes at the top of its class? Not always! Consider for a moment the role of the reserves team, for any of the major UK soccer teams. They also have a role to assist the return to full fitness, an injured first team player. An injured player will lack match practice, and they can only get match practice when they are able to play with the reserves, until he is fit enough to play a full game in the first team.

It is the job of the manager of the reserves to make room for these first team players who are on the injured list. The manager will know, not only is practice important, but at the same time the need to limit their match practice according to the advice of the physiotherapist, trainer and doctor. This is something which rarely happens in the business world, but it might be a team member in the business world needs to come back to the team slowly after a major illness.

In business we also need to understand the role of the team and the length of time the team will be together. It's no good thinking what a team specifically set in place to develop a new computer system, which consists of programmers; systems analysts; and representatives from the departments, where the systems will be used, will continue to be in place after the system is completed and accepted by the company.

This type of team will be broken up, you will find any freelance consultants will go on their way and the permanent staff will probably be the backbone of any support and development team for the new computer system.

It might be as simple as bringing in a new computer package or operating system to the company. Windows 7 is going to be the next Microsoft operating system. However, there is one difference between Windows 7 and all the other operating systems Microsoft has brought out. Windows 7 is promised to run on the same hardware which would run Windows Vista.

Does it make a difference? Yes it means the hardware costs are reduced for the new operating system. Every other operating system has always required an upgrade to the hardware as well as the software. The failure of Vista to appear on computers for so many years, as well as its failure to capture the hearts and minds of those who buy computers has something to do with this change.

We have seen the appearance of Netbooks (small portable computers) and Nettops (small desktop computers) which has helped Microsoft to realize the majority of computer users do not need more and more power to perform day-to-day tasks.

For most of those who need extra PC power to enable spreadsheets for them to do their calculations, have found it was possible to have performed the same arithmetic on a mini-computer or a mainframe computer. You should remember in business most of the number-crunching is no more complex than arithmetic (add, subtract, multiply, and divide), with some statistical analysis but not very much. The only time this is not the case is when a company is involved in complex statistical analysis.

When it comes to defining the role of your team you need to be quick and to the point. Give yourself two minutes to clearly portray what your team does. Some people might ask you to do this in 60 seconds or less. It is difficult to do, but often you may be put on the spot by a new manager or director to see if you fit into the organization. Once you understand and can verbalize the role of your team in the organization, you can communicate this information to your team (if it is a new team). This exercise will ensure you are focused on what the team is about, and being able to state clearly and precisely what the team stands for. It is a skill you need to master, and one which the saying is true, "Practice makes perfect."

In the event of you becoming a manager of an existing team, you should take the time to check with the team, because you need to understand the major role of the team, and you need to ensure it's not complicated by some minor roles which you also play. Often your senior manager will not communicate the minor roles unless your team fails to accomplish them.

In Organization

We've looked at the clarity needed to have for the aims and goals of the organization as whole. We've looked at the company tag line and mission statement. Now we'll need to see where the work is allocated to your team fits into the whole of the company.

If the company is multi-national it might be complicated, and you should take time to ask the questions of your manager. However, it will always be necessary to see how the team fits into the geographical environment of the company.

For most USA-based teams it will be necessary to find out how the team fits into the whole of the USA. If you are based in Europe it could be necessary to find out how the company functions in your respective country, but also how it fits into other parts of Europe or even the whole of the EU. Knowing this will enable you to find the managers and directors whom you'll need to relate to within your company.

In Function

In a large organization, you need to remember what your team does will affect other teams and maybe the whole of the organization. Processing an order today or leaving it until tomorrow can be the difference between having a satisfied customer who might become a long term customer, and someone who is dissatisfied because it has taken too long to get the item purchased.

It only takes a company to supply one defective machine to a magazine writer or an industry commentator for one delivery to become a major issue for public relations. We are all in the business and are in control of the destiny of the company we are employed by. What we do or don't do will make a difference; make sure your all team members know how important each person is.

For the team leader there is the need to understand the flow of information to your team and from your team. The need is to understand the "pinch points" of the information flow to your team and from your team. Understand where you are going and how you are going to accomplish the work your team has to perform. A good team communicates, and always remember communication is two way. This is the secret of having a team which works well together.

Get Goals/Set Goals

In discussion with your manager or supervisor you'll need to get the goals which have been set for both you and your team. There can be a conflict in the way you allocate those goals to individuals. You'll need to remember most team members will need to be flexible, which will allow them to cover all the work every day of the week, and every week of the year.

There is an enormous contrast with a soccer team. Let's look at the basic positions which are in a soccer team, you have the forwards; midfield; defenders and goalkeeper. The forwards will normally support each other. But, the midfield players need to do their own work, and also support the forwards during an attack and the defenders when needed to defend. The defenders will support their goalkeeper and also the rest of the team when a corner is taken in the opponents half. The goalkeeper will be playing as a solo player because he is finally responsible for the defense of the goal. But, look how every member of the team has an important role, and you'll find the team which wins the game is also those who played the game as a team.

The same situation is in the business world. Everyone needs to be working together to complete the whole task of the business or soccer team.

Discuss The Goals With Your Manager

Having set the goals, you'll need to do a revision of the goals with your manager. This is to ensure there is nothing missing in the goals which you had set, and also to keep the goals relevant and changed as the company changes. Your manager will need to set the balance between the major goals and the minor ones before you allocate them to your team. It is essential to get the balance between the main goals and the minor goals, because you don't want to focus on the wrong goals, or have your team members making the decision to work on a goal because they prefer one over another goal.

Review Goals After Discussion With Your Manager

One of the problems a manager faces is when they are given tight deadlines. The temptation is to rush to get a project started, and then find you have to retract or reorganize, because you didn't review the goals before starting. You'll need to take your time to locate and organize what the team needs to do. It might seem some of your time will be taken doing this, but it will save you a lot of time in the overall time spent on the project.

Communicate Goals To The Team

This will be a task which will be necessary to do on a regular basis. In many ways, when you look at soccer, the manager has the easy job – his pep talk before the match and at half time is expected of all the team members. Yet to give a business team a pep talk every day or every half day would very quickly become counter-productive. You will need a regular discussion of how well the team is going with their goals is far more effective. Use your time to motivate and congratulate the team as well.

Get Team To Communicate Those Goals

The goals of your team must become part of them, enabling them to be able to communicate them to new team members and also to those who have been part of the team for any length of time. Shared goals and shared values need to go from the mind to the heart. It seems like an 18 inch journey physically but changes the whole attitude of the individual to the goals, which they have not only accepted but taken as their own goals. The difference is seen when the team member comes into work every day.

It is the same when the soccer player steps on

the pitch wearing the strip of his new team. He could be playing against his former club but he will take the instructions from the new manager and the passes to and from his new teammates. It is often difficult when a player is transferred between two teams in the same league, but he knows where his loyalties now belong, to the new team who are paying his wages. This is the challenge which faces any manager who has agreed a transfer of a player from one team in the same league to your team. Changing the mental and heart allegiance from the old team to the new one could just be the most difficult thing a manager has to do.

Publicly Recognize Those Who Have Shown Commitment To The Goals

You may be the only team in your company, or the only team in your league to hold your own awards and recognition ceremony. The year may have been a good or a bad one for the company but still we need to recognize the performers within the team. Sometimes it's not necessary to give someone a booby prize, just seeing how the people are who receive a public recognition of their contribution to the team's work will spur on the under-achievers to get the recognition next time.

Inform Your Manager Of Your Star Players

This may already be part of the annual staff assessment process, if not; you should make a point to recommend the stars on your team. If the worst comes to the worst they will get promoted before you do, and you'll have to train someone else to take their place. Why is this worst? Because you will lose a good team member, yet you will also get a tremendous satisfaction in seeing one of your team reaching their full potential. Be careful not to let your ego get in the way of saying the truth about this person. Otherwise, you will block the progress of your team members. You will always find some who have the potential to rise up the corporate ladder and achieve far more than you can ever achieve.

Chapter 2 Chosen By Default

2009 is a time when a new President has been chosen in the United States. A new President has chosen the team of people who will support him through the start of his administration. However, the President doesn't have a free hand to choose the people whom he would like to be on his team.

Each of the members of the President's team has to face the questions of the Senators and Representatives before they can take office. There are always those who will fail to come through this process. At times it might seem the President has taken second best. It is only after seeing how they serve the team, will you really know if the best was chosen. Hindsight is 20-20 vision and often this is needed to understand whether the best has been chosen.

In some ways, it doesn't matter what team you lead, because you don't always get exactly what you would want. In the same way, an entrepreneur may find the right candidate to fill a position, and then the candidate demands too high a salary for his services. The crucial point is to know this is about being a team, and building a team which works together. In business people might not have the luxury of a separate group of people who will make the decision, they will have to make a decision themselves, and then see how each team player plays.

An Existing Team

On a football field it is easy to visualize the team dynamics. We shall start by considering a team strategy based on 4; 4; 2; - 4 defenders; 4 midfield players and 2 forwards.

The organization is for the central defenders to

play the ball forward to the central midfield players and then to the two forwards. Similarly, the left defenders play forward to the left midfield players and then to the forwards.

When a new manager arrives to take over an existing team the dynamics are not always so clear cut. Often, it is difficult for the manager to discern the difference between the real leaders within his new team and those who follow. It is a skill which many new managers have yet to learn, how to discern; and to know the difference between those who understand the work flow and those who are following what they are told without really understanding why they do any task.

A Team Chosen For You

You will always find there are times in business where you are either moved or hired to manage a brand new team. No-one else has been found who can do the job, but the need of the task to be accomplished means the team was chosen before you arrived. On a soccer team this could mean a complete set of misfits with goalkeepers, midfield players and forwards either in short supply or oversubscribed.

In business you will have to deal with the different personalities, those who want to be part of the team, but only if they don't have to make any decisions. You will also have those who want to have their own way and make all the decisions. Either of these situations can cause friction, and people can easily lose their temper because of feeling they are not being listened to.

A soccer player-manager can fulfill some of the roles which are vacant, but they are unable to do it all the time. You should find how a new team must be able to communicate well together and this will enable them to quickly start to knit together as a team, rather than individuals.

This is something you have to do when you are the manager. There are specific things you can do which will help. It could be taking the time to have various social gatherings, meals together is a great way of getting people relaxed, and being able to share one with the other. It is important for team members to be given every opportunity to get to know the other team members and then be able to partner with them.

Being a good manager you will know your team, or you will take the time to know your team. Imagine for a moment, your team loves to go bowling, what would be easier, trying to build a team in the workplace, or arranging an evening where the team goes bowling, followed by a meal in a local restaurant. A good manager won't have to tell the people it is about team building; the people will go and enjoy the event because it doesn't seem like work. How many times have you been in the office when someone says, let's all go out for lunch? It happens often, and again it's a way of building and strengthening the team.

Don't you find it is always nice to be able to put a face with a name especially when talking on the telephone? It is always helpful to start to learn about them and how they will react in any situation, will they remain calm or will they panic quickly?

These social gatherings can be very difficult for the person who doesn't work for the business, but is invited as partners have been included. Your partner even though they might enjoy meeting and putting faces to the names, may not fit in with the team on an educational, social, political, or spiritual level. So make the effort with partners to connect and at least talk to them.

One of the roles you will have as the manager is to ensure everyone feels at home and welcomed. This might move you out of your comfort zone, but you will find it most rewarding, if you are able to encourage everybody, whether they are team members or not.

A Luxury – You Choose

Is this a luxury? Yes. There are a number of times when a team leader comes in from the outside the company, and starts as the new employee, as there is no-one in terms of age, experience and length of service within the company which can distinguish the existing team members from one another. In simple terms there is no natural leader within the group, and the choice is to take one person and promote them with the likelihood of jealousy and bad relationships, or bring in someone from outside with the need to build relationships from scratch. The advantage for the new person is the understanding they are brought in to manage, and are an unknown, until the team gets to know them, they are safe. Once the team gets to know them there is the danger of them being told they are not a suitable leader.

Who would you choose as your "Dream Team?" A man may choose to have his office filled with beautiful women, and a woman may choose handsome men, but what if an accident or incident robs them of their beauty? The soccer manager may choose a team full of the most expensive star players in the world, but will they play together as a team, or will they only do what they want to do. What about all the times when David Beckham and other stars of the soccer world have been criticized for not working as part of the team, but solely working to do their little part of the play which will brings them the limelight and the glory?

The manager must consider the whole of the team and how to strengthen it. This may be a training course in a business environment, or a new fitness regime to increase the strength or suppleness of a soccer player. There may be a good reason why you cannot hire a new team member, but until you are aware of the weaknesses of the team as a whole you cannot reorganize to make the most of your strengths and minimize your weaknesses.

Chapter 3 Team Analysis

It doesn't matter the size of the team, you should always be analyzing it from every angle to understanding the way it works and most importantly why it fails.

10-80-10

Did you know 10% of your team will be positive leaders rooting for you and the team objectives? 80% of the team will be followers who can be influenced in the way they follow. The final 10% are negative leaders trying to draw the team away under their leadership to accomplish their own set of goals and aims. Now for a small team the percentages may vary a little but seeing people in their 3 roles as supportive leader, follower and negative leader may help you to understand why the team dynamics are as they are, and why the team refuses to follow you.

Male/Female

In sports teams it is often easy with each sport potentially having male and female leagues and teams. When this happens you'll find you do not have the mix of male and female on the same team.

In business it is totally different with workplaces split with men and women working together. With a mixed team the "locker room humor" which can be heard on the sports field is inappropriate and needs to be avoided at all costs. We can all remember the new manager who brought all his extended team together and his way of introducing himself was crude and it offended most of the women who were included in the team.

It might have been his aim to see who would be offended but it quickly becomes counter-productive. In a mixed team the dynamics of the team are affected by the males being protective of the women on the team, and the women's maternal instincts coming to the fore when dealing with the younger men. Also, on a mixed team there is always the possibility of there being a romance or two. However, should the couple breaks up or there is rivalry between two women or two men the whole team can shatter and become unworkable. Many companies have very strict rules about romantic relationships in the workplace. For hardworking people there are often very few places where they can safely seek out a partner, and there are times when people do get married as a result of a relationship in work.

Enthusiasm vs. Experience

Should we say youth vs. experience? No, as there are times when an older person can become very enthusiastic about a new team of people, some new technology or task at a company. There needs to be a balance in every team. Often the manager will provide a great deal of the experience, but there are times when the individual team member will be looked to by other team members for their experience.

Religion

While it is illegal to discriminate against someone on the basis of religion in the US & UK when you are employing them, you can find people of different religions can cause problems within the team you are managing. You will find you need to take a great deal of care, when views are expressed by the minority, and you want to avoid any anger by the majority.

Events take place around the world, where different religions are in conflict with each other. If a member of your team feels strongly about the world events, then it can also cause problems with the other team members.

Religion is a topic which many companies encourage their employees not to talk about, they know how a calm discussion, can become a heated debate, with both sides wanting the final word. Not only will you have different religious groups wanting to talk about their beliefs, but they will also want to make it clear their views on many hot topics. Abortion; homosexuality; pre-marital sex; couples living together, will all invoke strong reactions, but the reality is even though people have differing views they can work together, and become a strong and successful team. Every team member needs to know they have a safe environment to discuss topics and come to the agreement of being able to agree to disagree at times.

However, if one person demands everyone change and become like them, you will start to see tensions within the team, especially is the person demanding change is the manager. Personal beliefs have to stay outside the team, unless the team is being asked to do something which is outside a member's belief system.

Marital Status

When you have a team which comprises of singles, they will socialize together far more than a team full of married people regardless of whether they have or don't have children. It can be very difficult for the non-team partner to come along to a social event and then to fit in to the group, especially if they haven't met them before, and feel they have nothing in common. Also, if the majority of your team members are married, you will find their availability to work, or train over and above the normal working hours could be limited. You will also need to consider those team members who are single parents, and how it will affect the dynamics of the team should their child/children be taken sick.

Technical Ability

When you play soccer, the one thing the

manager doesn't normally do is to put the goal keeper to play as a striker. There are times when you will put a player into a position they don't normally play, but when you face an emergency, you have to know which of your players can cover for that time. Later we will look at the story of a midfielder who played a great deal of a match in goalie position during an English FA Cup match.

We normally play the game according to people's technical ability. Forward, winger, midfield player, back, goalkeeper. The same is true in a business. When you have someone who is a good graphic designer, you'll find them jobs where they can use their skills and talents. A person, who excels at writing, can be working on adding the content to a website. Different people to cover different tasks will ensure the jobs are completely quickly and easily. When you find you are restricted by the size of the team, you will then have people multi-tasking and some people will have to move outside their comfort zone. The advantage of this is, some people will discover gifts and talents they didn't know they had. They might even look to diversify when the project is completed, because they enjoyed a specific task and found where their talents lie.

Star Test

A "star" can either be a liability or an asset. Often, this is more a soccer issue and not often a business problem.

When you think of soccer, a name which most people know is Maradona who was an excellent soccer player. He played for Argentinos Juniors, Boca Juniors, FC Barcelona, and Napoli. The incident which brought him a great deal of negative comment over the years happened during the 1986 World Cup.

It was 4 years after the Falklands war, where

Britain and Argentina fought over the Falklands Islands. When these two teams played each other in the FIFA World Cup emotions were running high.

The first score was from Maradona after 51 minutes and the referee missed Maradona handling the ball in the area to score the goal. Maradona also scored one more goal during the match, and it was credited as the Goal of the Century.

Gary Lineker scored a goal for England, but the final score was 2-1 to Argentina. Argentina went on to win the tournament. After the match, Maradona didn't admit to handling the ball in the attack, and he said, "It was the "hand of god."" It was 22 years later when Maradona apologized for the handball in an interview with the UK "Sun" newspaper.

Flexibility Test

Do you know how flexible your team members are? Are they caught inside the box; they refuse to do anything which might stretch them, because they are afraid of failure? Are the members of your team willing to operate in different roles within the team, and within the organization?

It might be difficult for some teams to allow for any flexibility, but it should be attempted, and there should be cross training and mutual support.

An example of this was Glen Hoddle, when he played soccer for Tottenham Hotspur. Hoddle was an attacking midfielder; he was 6ft tall, which made him an obvious player on the field.

The memorable day was January 9th 1990. Disaster struck when the goalkeeper for Tottenham, Milija Aleksic suffered a broken jaw during an FA Cup match against Manchester United. It was a replay match, and one which was crucial for Spurs to win.

This was in the days when most teams didn't have any reserve keepers on the bench. Hoddle stepped up and took over the goalkeeping for the remainder of the match. The match went to extra time, because the team played as a team, they did everything possible to keep the opposing side from the goal. They did all they could to protect Hoddle in his new position. Spurs went on to win the tie during extra time. (Hoddle also took over in goal in two other matches. One was in October 1979 when Barrie Daines was injured in a game against Leeds United and again in December 1980 when Milija Aleksic was injured again.) Here was a man who trained and worked as an attacking midfielder, and yet was will to take over in goal and see his side become triumphant.

Take time to discover how flexible your team is when it comes to helping one another, especially when there is an emergency, or when something goes wrong?

Away Days

Have you thought about having an "away day" for your team? The costs of corporate away days might seem to be expensive, but the real benefits with understanding the way people are motivated is priceless.

There are many options for "away days" and you should consider the people on your team when you make the final decision about how this team building exercise will work. If it is too aggressive, you risk alienating people, but if you have a "Spa Day" you might find some people not enjoying themselves as well.

When people are faced with many of the activities on these team building days, you will always find those who react with fear, and trepidation. They don't want to be involved, and it is your job to encourage them and help them to overcome their fear.

It might mean incorporating some simple team games, where people have to rely on their partner to get to the end of the task. A person, who is blindfolded, will need precise and clear instructions from their partner to get past any obstacles in their way. This is a great way to build a rapport with people, and will encourage even the shyest and most timid member of your team to see they have something to offer the team.

It might be for some people their competitive instincts come out, and they may reveal some unexpected traits, and talents which they didn't realized they had. But, also you will find for some people the most important part of the day, was seeing their self confidence being built. When someone who assumes they can't do anything new, suddenly finds the opposite is true, you will end up with a much stronger team member, who is now prepared to take a risk, and work for the good of the team.

SWOT And SMART Analysis

These analysis acronyms are normally used to analyze a business as a whole, but many of them are also applicable to teams regardless of whether they are part of a business or a sports team.

SWOT

SWOT encourages the entrepreneur or manager to analyze their business on the basis of four factors.

- Strengths
- Weaknesses

- Opportunities
- Threats

This analysis can be applied at both individual and at a team level. What are the strengths of the person or team when it comes to accomplishing the task which has been set? Often, people will like to talk about their strengths, but you have to be aware of over confidence, which can also cause problems within the team.

What are the weaknesses? Weakness is a subject which many people try and avoid talking about. They feel if they were to admit to a weakness, their colleagues and other team members would look negatively at them. Yet, knowing what the weaknesses are is crucial if you are to win as a team, and being able to turn those weaknesses into strengths is something many teams don't do.

How do opportunities affect us? There are opportunities to score goals, or to complete a task or even part of a task. There are opportunities all around us, and yet if you look firmly at the closed box, you will miss many of these. Often, people think they can't take an opportunity because they feel other people will also be trying to get the same contract, or take the same opportunities. This might be true, but if you never try and take the opportunities presented to you, you will never, ever know what you are capable of achieving.

What threats are there to completing the task? Do you have the best goal-scorer in the league, the best defender or the best goalkeeper? In business the Opportunities and Threats may not be as clear-cut as they are to the soccer team, but we still need to evaluate them. Threats are all around in business, but knowing what the threat is, will enable you to present your business and team in a different way to the opposition.

SMART

When looking at SMART you need to take five factors into account when looking at a team or business. We must have goals for the team which are Specific, Measurable, Achievable, Realistic, and Timed.

The goal to be the best team in your particular league and to remain in the league or to gain promotion to the next league is a great goal. However, you will find it isn't a specific goal. You will see there is no time period for accomplishing the goal.

Let's imagine you have the worst team around, and you are without major finance (for a business or professional team) or enormous dedication (for the amateur team) this goal will not be accomplished this year or next.

The specific means you aim to be the best in 3 years and during the time you need to be in the top 10 after 1 year, the top 3 in 2 years and the top 1 in the third year. Now we are talking specific.

We also need measurable goals. We need to know how many points we will have, how many goals we will score, and the maximum number of goals we will concede. This is measurable performance.

Achievable can be relatively easy to evaluate in a business setting. If you have sold 2,000 items last year then 2,500 may be easily achievable unless you have only sold 2,000 items for each of the last 10 years.

Realistic can look good on paper, but does it seem completely realistic when submitted to the bank manager (for a business owner) or to the board of a sports club. You will find some people can be very hard-headed when it comes to making decisions about the future prospects of a club or business.

Timed is something we all need to understand. It is no good being the top of the league at Christmas only to crash out and be in the middle at the end of the season. Can this happen? Yes, especially when there is insufficient cash in the club and the accounts books can only be balanced by selling your star players.

Take a look at Swansea City, they are not one of the world's best know soccer clubs. However, in the 1977/1978 they were in the fourth division (only four divisions existed in the English football league) which meant they were in the bottom league.

In each of the next 3 seasons they were promoted and by the 1981/1982 season they played in the First Division and topped the league several times during the season, and finally finished 6th.

Yet, the story doesn't have a good ending. Due to financial problems in the club, the race up the leagues was followed by being demoted from the leagues and at the end of the 1985/1986 season they were relegated back to the fourth division.

Today the Swans play in League Division 1 (the top league is now the Premier League). On the one hand you must never say never, but on the other hand your aims as a team must be viewed in terms of the SWOT and SMART analysis.

Chapter 4 Team Dynamics

Every team member is different. Every team is different. Some teams can be consistent day after day and week after week. Other teams need to have the manager leading by example, and giving exactly what is needed at each stage of the game. This is one of the first jobs you need to do as a team manager, get to know your team, and see what the differences are with each team member.

Communicate Face-To-Face

Sometimes this is easier said than done. What happens if your star player has to be out for a day, because they are signing autographs and making personal appearances? The companies they are being sponsored by expect these appearances to be made to promote their company as well.

A text message is not enough to communicate

what he needs to work on during the next day before a big game. Towards the end of the season in Europe, the weeks get very congested for the top clubs. You'll find there are normal week-by-week league games. However, there are times when they have to play extra games to catch up, especially after bad weather in January and February.

You will have the country-based cup games. And not forgetting the cup games for Europe and these involve a home and an away leg. The more you play at the top, the more congested the fixture list becomes, and the more difficult it is to adequately rest players between matches.

You will then need to add into the equation, the pressure which comes, there will be the requirement of players to play for their own country team and be away for that time. There are local championships such as European,

American and Asian competitions for countries, and also the World Cup, without the necessity of qualifiers. Your star player or players may be the right one for their country as well, but the pressure on you, as the manager, is to continue to get results for your club. You need to be able to communicate face to face.

The same is true for the business team. Face to face communication may be difficult when the team manager is on one continent (e.g., America) and the team is on another continent (e.g., Europe or Asia). This is when you should be making use of Skype, which will enable you to see the person you are talking to, even if you need to call him or her at home in order to have some privacy. Nothing beats talking face to face as often as possible. Only then will the person tend to open up to you, rather than hiding behind the mask, when they say what they think you need to hear.

Full-Time Management

The names of the full-time soccer managers can trip off the tongue. It doesn't matter if it is Arsène Wenger (Arsenal); Sir Alex Ferguson (Manchester United); or Guus Hiddink (Chelsea). You may prefer the US soccer team head coaches as they do not seem to have the team managers who exist in the UK and Europe, Dennis Hamlett (Chicago Fire); Steve Nicol (New England Revolution); and Preki Radosavljevic (Club Deportivo Chivas USA).

These men all face the week-by-week and game-by-game team management problems and successes. They might not have the medical knowledge of any medical condition and injuries their players face, but on their team they will have a qualified person who is advising them. In some ways sports managers have enormous advantages over the managers of other businesses, but they also have enormous disadvantages.

The advantages are, when a player has an injury, you will find there is always part of the year where matches are not played. During this time it is possible for players to be operated on, and also to receive much needed time for rest and recuperation. Changes can be made to the playing surface and the stadium. If there are problems and they can be rectified. However, there are no let-offs in business.

The disadvantages in soccer are everyone is under intense scrutiny for 90 minutes (more if there is extra time). All the criticism comes from the team's actions during the game. It often doesn't take into consideration the health of the players, or the pressures the player's face from birth, death and general life. It is all down to how they perform during the span of ninety minutes. Once it is all over the fans, and the people go home, but the players, the manager and the other members of the management team need to keep going and be motivated for the next game.

Part-Time Management

When Bob Bradley took over from Bruce Arena as the US national soccer team manager they faced the problems of being part-time team managers. It isn't they were working part-time as a team manager, but their players play in a number of soccer clubs all over the world, every week.

The national manager faces the problem of soccer clubs who may not want their "injured" player to take part in an international match before he is fully recovered. The battle for availability and flexibility means most national team managers must spend an enormous amount of time reviewing all the players who are showing potential to become part of the international squad.

For the international soccer team manager who is bringing the squad together for Copa America or the World Cup, it is relatively easy as the whole team will be together for a number of weeks. Yet, for the qualifying matches they are only together for a few days at most.

The experience of playing in a team where you may not know the strengths and weaknesses of your team mates, or you might be playing against members of your own week-by-week team, can be daunting especially the first time you are part of this new squad. Add into this mix the completely different styles of playing in different countries, and you'll have a challenge for all the players, especially the new ones.

For the part-time soccer manager keeping in contact with his players and evaluating both their fitness and injuries is almost a full-time job in its own right. When you also realize they have to evaluate the new players and the enormous schedule of international soccer matches, you will realize how big a job they really have to do.

In contrast, a manager within a business may have the same situation of being a full-time employee, yet some or all of the team members are working on other projects, or other parts of the business. Negotiations between the part-time manager and the line manager of the team members, which will allow team meetings, can take an enormous amount of time. Frustrations are unavoidable but must not be allowed to affect the progress of the work which needs to be done.

Project Team

In some ways the project team mentality is almost like a national soccer team being away from their normal day-to-day club to concentrate on a particular competition. The differences begin to emerge as the soccer competition has an end date, even if you manage to play in the finals, but the project team could be caught up in changes to business, technology or architecture for months or even years at a time.

The advantage of a project team is it has a well-defined start, a goal to aim for and a well-defined end. This enables the work to be carried out in a methodical way and you have a well-aimed project. The disadvantages are, the need to bring together the team quickly and progress the project to completion.

Chapter 5 Day By Day Difficulties

We all face problems cause through day-by-day living, and being part of a team doesn't lessen these problems. We can try to ignore any problems hoping they will go away, but they won't. When they are ignored you will find they will become more of a problem and not only hurt you as a manager, but also your team members will suffer.

Stress

Within some organizations they have peak activity seasons, where the organization must make a great deal of money or face the possibility of going bankrupt. There are many dangers, with stress catching up with people at such a time.

People react differently to stress, and you should be aware of how you team members will all be different and react differently. For some they might go out and get drunk. Others will take anti-depressants or happy-pills, which will enable them to get through periods such as the run-up to Christmas or Thanksgiving or Easter.

For other people it is a combination of factors. They have problems of sickness within their family, a heavy workload, financial pressure and demanding children all conspire to put an individual or a group of individuals under stress.

Stress can display in very many ways. Often stress is demonstrated in anger/hostility or outbursts of emotion which has no obvious cause in their visible environment.

Medical advice needs to be sought by the team member or team leader because you need to find ways which the stress can be limited and removed. For some people on your team you will need to find any medical treatment which may be needed. There are many drugs and homeopathic remedies which can be tried to see if the symptoms of stress can be reduced.

People find a hobby or taking some exercise help, and during the exercise period, endorphins will be released, which are a natural anti-depressant. How many will put on their MP3 player and listen to relaxing music? Under stress others will go for spa treatments, or a massage to relieve the physical stress of the situation they are in at this time. It is important to understand the person under stress has someone in the organization they can talk to without prejudice. One option is to cut down the number of hours worked in a week for a period, which will reduce the stress a person is dealing with.

You should remember stress will not just "go away" it will need to be treated and resolved. Always be aware of the problems and also the dangers of a person resorting to drugs, sex, alcohol or a mixture of all three.

Conflict

Whenever people work in close proximity or with urgent deadlines there is a great danger of conflict. Even when there is a relatively easy workload and no looming deadlines, people do not always work or play together well. Sometimes, you have to look at it in terms of there being a personality or ideology clash. Ideology can vary from different religions to clash between those who want to solve many of the world's problems with war, against those who feel all war is unacceptable. This can become a very heated debate.

Finally, there are people who are pro choice and those who are pro life in arguments about abortion. You also have those who want to allow homosexual marriages and those who are against them. Such attitudes generate a whole lot of feeling on both sides. The problem is for most people there is not much light being created on either side.

Between Team Members

Hopefully, the conflict doesn't degenerate into physical blows but in many of the debates in our cultures there are no real answers to both sides. When you look at the problems of war in the world, broadening the definition of marriage to include those who practice homosexuality, and the abortion debate, you will find some of the disputes are getting nowhere in terms of resolution.

A resolution of conflict between team members must be attempted as soon as possible. It is all very well thinking the storm will pass over, but as team leader you'll need to stop the conflict spreading and you should try to reconcile the two or more combatants. In the end it may be necessary for them to agree, they will continue to hold different views, and not fight within the office environment. At worst it may be necessary either to transfer one of the combatants to another team or they may need to leave the company. It is hard when it comes it happens but sometimes you must "play nicely."

It can be even worse when a soccer team is split apart by the actions and attitude of two of their team members. It can be as simple as team members arguing over who takes a free kick as happened on March 10th 2009 when Leeds United played Yeovil Town. Not an important match, but a problem of attitude which teaches our children bad attitudes when they play soccer. You can read stories all the time of players speak bad things about their team mates and you realize they have done it purely for the publicity. Where does it get them? Nowhere!

Between Yourself And One Or More Team Members

The bigger problem faced by many managers is when a team member tries to attack you either personally or for what you are doing as a manager. It may be they think you are biased for them or against them, but it doesn't matter which. The first priority is to stop the rot spreading.

If one person is complaining it will not take much time before all the team is complaining about you and the way you do things. You need to take action and stop the rot; you need to deal with the person before they set the whole team against you. Talk it through and work out a solution if possible. If this is not possible then a transfer to another team or the person leaving the company is essential.

Safety

Companies have different policies in regard to safety, and you will find their attitude to safety can change depending on who you talk to. Some companies are extremely lax, whereas, others are extremely rigid. One of the things you should do is to check how often safety inspections are carried out.

You need to be involved pro-actively in ensuring the area which your team occupies within the premises is both safe and clean. This might mean enlisting the help of a member of your team who is of the opposite sex to check out their toilets to ensure they are clean.

It is an area of importance because if the toilets are not clean, you will find diseases can spread easily. (As a note at this point I have usually found if the toilets are not clean and hygienic the company does not care much for its staff.

You should develop the habit of using a toilet on the site of an interview to check this out). The same when you walk around, not only near to the team's desks but also anywhere they walk, including the corridor to the coffee bar or machine and the way to the canteen. If there are any lapses in safety, you need to make sure they are dealt with immediately.

Sports teams have responsibilities, for the safety of their players. The more expensive the player the greater the cost is to play a game without him, while he takes the time recovers from a training injury. It is to avoid training injuries we must take care of the Astro Turf, or any other makes of artificial turf. We need to ensure players are wearing tracksuits. A slide on this artificial turf will cause a friction burn which will take time to heal.

Also, MRSA stays active longer in an artificial turf, which means it is essential to disinfect it to clear out any possibility of the infection getting into a wound or being spread to the rest of the team. These are a few examples but making sure the team is fit and stays fit right through the season is essential and injuries in and around the training field or the main stadium should be avoided.

Chapter 6 Delegation

There are distinct differences between the soccer pitch and business when it comes to delegation. Most of the time, a team on the soccer pitch is under the watchful gaze of the manager, either from the dugout or the stands. In business, however the work which the team members is doing may not be seen by the manager until the project is complete and the work is presented to them.

Delegate Responsibilities

Responsibilities are clear-cut on the soccer pitch. The goalkeeper is responsible for keeping a clean sheet (no goals allowed in) but he has the assistance of the defenders and sometimes the whole team. The forwards are responsible for scoring goals with midfielder players often assisting and scoring. It is sometimes the defender who has come forward for a corner or a free kick, who has the honor of scoring for his team.

The essential news is, the team must play and work as a team and never, ever give up on one another or the task ahead.

Within a business the help is often more verbal than practical, and can take place around a coffee break. For a business there may be the necessity of calling for technical help from the IT person or team in order to perform a task on the computer system. For example, a training course on PowerPoint or Impress may be a nice time for the team member until they have to use the training and prepare the slides for a presentation. It is easy to think you have made sense of the software while on a course, but it is totally different when months later you have to use the software for the first time. Try and ensure when someone goes on a training course they use the knowledge gained on the course, as soon as possible, especially when they return to the office.

Responsibilities may be shared around the team. For example one person may be responsible to give any help needed with a computer problem before the IT team or person is called in. This would be the most knowledgeable person in terms of the company's IT systems and programs.

Delegate Authority

The captain on the soccer pitch has the manager's authority. Should he be substituted or taken off injured, someone else has to take the captain's armband. The manager may continue to shout from the touchlines but he cannot be on the pitch making decisions at the same time.

There will always be a time in an office when the team manager will be away because of having to take sick leave or vacation. At these times a deputy can take over the team, and run everything under the delegated authority of the manager. There is however a second level of delegation which goes on in an office. In order to perform a task the manager delegates some of their authority in order to instruct how the job is done. The authority comes from the manager, but the actions are taken under the manager's authority by the team member. We often see both levels of authority being delegated by the manager of a team to an individual and to a deputy.

Trust Them

Here is one of the biggest challenges for the manager of a team. Can I trust my team to work to the best of their capabilities when I am not around? It is the old problem of what happens to a class when the teacher is not around. It often descends into chaos with everyone doing as they like. For a soccer team the assistant manager may keep order. For a team in business the deputy may not have known about the absence of their manager until too late to get organized.

Chapter 7 Disasters

One old TV program used to have the slogan "Expect the unexpected." For a manager the test of managing a disaster and coming out the other side of the problem with your position either intact or strengthened is a major one.

The Judas Test – 2 Betrayals In One Night

Yes, we are using this example which is from the Bible, but this is management at the very heart of a deep crisis of confidence. Jesus of Nazareth was betrayed twice in the matter of hours. Once by Judas, as he was the treasurer of his team.

For a long time Judas had his "hand in the till" taking money which belonged to Jesus and his team of disciples. Now he took the opportunity to get some more money by betraying Jesus. What Judas thought isn't going to be debated, because we don't know if he thought Jesus would escape as he had so many times before, or what he thought. Judas has always been known as the betrayer. Later, while Jesus was being interrogated Peter, one of the most trusted of Jesus team denied he even knew Jesus. Peter was in the wrong place at the wrong time and it was obvious by his accent, which showed he was from Galilee.

Every team leader will eventually face betrayal. It is not any good avoiding it or covering it up. Someone will leave the team taking with them important knowledge and information which they then share with their new employer. Or maybe someone will speak to a senior manager to betray a confidence about you or an indiscretion which you have committed or seem to have committed.

Judas hung himself

This is a tragic end to the man who made a decision to betray his team leader. He decided he had done wrong. He went back to the Jewish authorities and tried to put it right. When his attempts to pay for what he did was rejected by those who tempted him to do wrong he went out and killed himself.

Peter became a great leader

One verse in the Bible makes the position clear (Luke 23:34) "Jesus and Peter (also called Simon) met together." What are the details of the meeting? We have only the fact of their meeting and not their conversation. Afterwards, though Peter became the leader of the team.

What was the difference between the two? Judas tried to pay for his betrayal by paying for it with money and it never works. Peter met with his manager face to face and they dealt with the betrayal. Over and over again we need to realize our team members are people and not machines. They feel, they hurt and they need time to interact with you one on one. These meetings may be the hardest you will face as a manager, but they will be the most productive if you deal with it properly.

One thing you may find profitable is to study the team leadership of Jesus by reading the Gospel of Mark. See how the disciples are trained, their thinking was challenged, and then sent out to put into practice what they had heard and they were trained again. Look how they are never allowed to settle back and be comfortable, because there is always something new to learn and understand.

Death – The Busby Babes

Success is a two-edged sword. One minute you

are on top of the world then disaster strikes. Nothing can illustrate this more than the situation which the Manchester United soccer team in February 1958 faced. The team had been playing in the European Cup in Belgrade. They were one of the best UK teams, and their manager was Matt Busby. Because the team was all young men, they were given the nickname the Busby babes.

At that time the aircraft were piston engine and this one had two engines. It didn't have the range of today's jet aircraft. The flight had to stop in Munich to refuel. After two attempts at taking off after the refueling, the aircraft crashed on the third attempt. Initially the pilots were blamed but the final evaluation found there was too much slush on the runway, and the aircraft failed to take off as it hit all this slush.

In the crash 21 of the 44 people on the plane were killed. The Manchester United club secretary, chief coach and the trainer were killed along with seven of the players. An eighth player died fifteen days later. Matt Busby was injured and was unable to return to manage the team during the season. Two players were injured and never played again. It left seven surviving players out of nineteen who started the journey.

Busby's injuries were so severe, he had to spend 2 months in hospital and was read the last rites twice. For a long time while he convalesced in Switzerland, Matt Busby wanted to quit. He was finally convinced to go back and rebuild the team when his wife told him, the players who had died would not have wanted him to quit.

This might be an extreme example, but most of us know someone who was cut off in their prime by a car, motorcycle or other accident. We can be very careful but one slip can be serious enough to take us out of the team.

Off The Pitch

We have all been saddened by the scenes of people crushed in the World Cup soccer match in Ivory Coast. Before Ivory Coast played Malawi a wall collapsed at the stadium. 22 people were killed and more than 130 injured. This happened in March 2009.

People being crushed at soccer matches are not unusual. The problem comes when people get killed. In the case of Liverpool the problem has happened to them twice but never at their home ground.

In 1985, Liverpool was at the top of the English leagues, and they were playing Juventus in the European Cup Final. The Final was held at the Heysel Stadium in Brussels. The problems were caused before the match started by hooligans trying to have a battle with the Juventus fans.

The Juventus fans tried to retreat, put pressure on a retaining wall and the wall collapsed. 39 people died and over 200 were injured. The match was played once the injured had been taken away. It led to British clubs being banned from European competitions for an indefinite period. The ban was lifted for the 1990-1991 season with Liverpool being banned for a further season.

In 1989 the FA cup semi-finals were held at the Hillsborough stadium of Sheffield Wednesday. The match was between Liverpool and Nottingham Forest. The match was abandoned after 6 minutes of the first half when fans were being crushed against fencing. 94 people died on the day and two more died in the next few days. There were 766 injured including 300 who needed hospital treatment. The subsequent inquiry led to major changes for clubs playing in the football league with all-seater stadium being required. Liverpool went

on to win the FA Cup final in 1989 against
Everton by 3 goals to 2 after extra time.

The question is with these two disasters facing
Liverpool, how do you encourage the team
when soccer fans have died, because they were
supporting their club? There are no simple
answers. Each team is unique and their
motivation is different. For many it would have
to be, you know the fans would not have
wanted you, their heroes to quit. To just keep
training, let alone playing is a battle and will
take the leadership of the manager and all the
staff. It is their reaction in the days and weeks
which follow a disaster, which will shape the
team for years to come.

War

War can be a time of enormous disasters. It
may be some members of your team get called
up for active service. After the World Cup in
1978 Tottenham Hotspur managed to hire

Osvaldo Ardiles (nicknamed "the python" in Argentina). Osvaldo was a great asset to Tottenham and he was joined by Ricky Villa in the midfield. The disaster was great for Tottenham Hotspur when war was declared between Argentina and Britain in 1982 and they both had to return home. Suddenly, Spurs went from having one of the best mid-fields in Britain to being very exposed by their two stars who were on the other side of the world. Today's idea is we can hire players from anywhere looks good on paper while the governments are friends, but falls apart when they are enemies.

Sickness

This can strike at any time. It can involve the team member or members of his family. Each person and each situation is different. Be flexible and support as much as you are able.

Father in intensive care after RTA

Things were going well in the IT department. There had been problems with one of the team leaders being an alcoholic but the company had dealt with the situation and the person had left the company.

It was all going well with a new IT manager changing the structure and bringing new opportunities. Then one evening a member of the IT team received the news from the Police then told him his father had been hurt in a traffic accident. Attempts to contact family near his home, which was over a hundred miles away, failed. The next morning after contacting a cousin he went to see his manager and was given time off.

His father was seriously ill. It took over two hours to drive home and the waiting started. He stayed over a week waiting. His father had suffered bruising to the brain and was not even recovering a level of consciousness. The doctors were concerned he had broken his back, but x-rays could not confirm it. The man returned to work as the father could have lived a long time on life support. The man went down to his home for Christmas, and two days after Christmas his father died. All through this time it affected the team. The telephone at this man's desk only had to click as a call was connected through and he was answering it.

Everyone was waiting for something positive but it did not come. The autopsy was performed and the father did have a broken spine, but the vertebra had popped completely out and had looked from straight on it was in a line, but from the side it was totally broken. In the end the man realized his father would have been a vegetable due to his brain injuries, and crippled from the waist down due to his spinal injuries. Neither his mother nor his father could have coped with the disability. All in all the nightmare lasted 20 days (December 7th to 27th) but it felt like a lifetime. Support for the man going through this is vital but the team will also be strained in unexpected ways and may react differently afterwards.

Child born blind

The pregnancy was normal, as far as everyone could tell. It was the second baby for this particular mother working with her team. The time came for her to finish work to begin the final preparations for the birth. Then the news came from the father, the baby had been born and was probably blind. It was a shock to everyone, especially to those close to her.

She was well known and well liked and questions were asked, "how could this have happened?" Now the time came for everyone to help. Her colleagues would need to be flexible when she returned to work as there would be further tests on the baby until she was much older. Was there any hope of her baby ever gaining her sight? Not according to the doctors. It was going to be an on-going problem for her to face for the rest of her life. We do not plan to bring a sick child into the world. We want healthy children but there are always a percentage of births where the baby has some sort of defect. Each case is different. Some necessitate the mother or father giving up work in order to look after the new child. Other problems necessitate flexible work arrangements as doctors and specialists do not work according to our time schedules.

Long-term sickness

In soccer the vast majority of players must be at the peak of their fitness and stamina. One person who broke the rule was Gary Mabbutt of Tottenham Hotspur.

You see Gary was a very versatile player, he mainly played in defense, but he also played as a midfielder. Gary however is a diabetic and has to inject himself with insulin to keep his blood in balance.

For Gary it was part of his every-day life and it did not prevent him having a very successful career at Bristol Rovers and he moved to Spurs where he became captain of the team. He won 16 caps playing for England. Gary played 16 years for the same team and when he retired he was the longest serving member of the soccer team. His diabetes has made him an icon for children and young people with diabetes, showing them no matter how hard their dreams may seem to be, go for it and get it.

Buying/Renting A New Home And Moving

It seems deceptively simple the first time you set up a home, with you either having bought or rented it. When you look back you realize why it is something which psychologists say is one of the three most stressful things you can face. (The three are buying/moving home, facing death of a close family member, and changing job. Indeed the psychologists will say to you, these three should not be done in the same year.) Sometimes the move is necessitated by accepting the new job but this is getting rarer in the current financial climate. From time to time every team will face one or more of its members moving and it does affect everyone. Sometimes a house move may turn into a team day out to help with the move into a new home. This action supports each other and it helps to build team spirit

Getting Married

It seems this is getting rarer these days as people live together but it does happen. This is one of those really stressful events. Getting all the families together and sitting down for a meal is enough, but when there can be three or four families involved it just multiplies the possibilities for conflict. How can there be this number of families? Simple the physical parents of one or both of the bride and the groom have divorced and remarried. If you add alcohol into the equation, we almost need to have a set of security guards available to keep "warring" families apart. Stress over what to wear, which people to invite, budgets, getting everything and everyone to the correct place at the correct time and so the lists of tasks go on. On the other hand there is the joy and excitement of an impending marriage. All in all, a wedding can have a very positive effect on the outlook of the team.

Having A Baby

We have already looked at the problem of a newborn baby who is sick. Here I want to look more generally at the nine months of preparing. The team may not know until later into the pregnancy, but the woman is affected even before she informs the rest of the team.

As a team manager you need to beware of health issues in the building especially when dealing with something like German measles, which will affect a baby in the womb. Also, the reaction of a pregnant woman could simply be to escape to her home and relative safety.

On one hand you'll find the joy of those around the woman, on another you'll find other women will look on at the pregnant women and want to get pregnant as they are "getting broody." For the manager there is one further issue, how is the team going to survive without this team member. This is an issue especially for a female soccer team, but also in business. However, when a man's partner is having a baby, there will be the time when the baby is born, and the man will need to spent time with his new family.

Adopting

The adoption process is long and complex with many highs and lows. The eventual outcome will be a child added to the family. For either potential adoptive parent they will have to go through a selection and training progress.

There will be conflicts between the parents' ideas of how a child should be raised, and the attitude of the so-called "experts." There will be the necessity of examining the possibilities of adopting a complete family, who have faced some traumatic experiences. The experience of having your lives and the lives of your parents put under scrutiny, especially if there have been any divorces is not comfortable. The couple will also find they have to face the examination of their financial status to ensure the child or children can be adequately cared for will take the couple outside their comfort zone. This can often spill over into the workplace as the continuing tensions and difficulties which have become part of their every day lives, outside of the workplace, means they can't escape the pressure.

Summary

People on your team will have a certain level of stress from their work situation. This stress increases enormously at times when external stress comes into the workplace. There is no doubt the economic changes in 2008/2009 have added to the stress in the workplace. You will need to be aware of people and their stress levels when allocating work. This is a skill you'll need to develop to know what the balance is, and only you can judge. Don't let the team member under stress simply sit there and contemplate the stress, but on the other hand do not overwhelm the team member with too much work, when they feel they can't cope. Balance is essential for the team workload.

Chapter 8 Cycles

All of life is lived in cycles. Even in our technologically-advanced society there are still cycles in life. Birth, growth and death are obvious as well as the seasons. Seasons may seem to be passing strangely, yet there remains the seasons of spring, summer, autumn, and winter. The seasons in soccer are also clear, but in a business environment it is not so clear-cut.

For A Sports Team – The Playing Season/ Rest And Recover

In the simplest environment you are either playing the sport or not, as the soccer season is fixed for playing. The manager and players must look at their year and evaluate their activities accordingly. It is all too easy to say soccer players in the top flight are under tremendous pressure and cannot use artificial stimulants such as alcohol after work.

In many ways the long-term progress (or failure) of a team is measured in a number of seasons put together. In the USA there is only a short term history. Teams such as Arsenal (founded in 1886 and joined the league in 1893) and Tottenham Hotspur (often called simply Spurs formed in 1882 and elected to the football league in 1908) have long histories in playing at the very top flight of the English football league. In these days of instant statistics from every match and every play, corner, and free kick, it still needs to be part of a longer-term strategy.

For the manager, he must have long-term goals and the means to accomplish those goals. This may mean the finance to buy players from some of the top soccer clubs in the world. It may mean being able to loan players to soccer clubs in other countries, which will build up the player's confidence in passing, ball-playing, scoring, and saving goals. The choice is usually a combination of buying and training. One of the weaknesses of the USA league at present is the low number of clubs. It is similar to the Scottish football league which is dominated by the two football clubs from Glasgow (Rangers and Celtic). The division of the city of Glasgow into two parts is very simple. The Celtic supporters are almost entirely Catholics, and the Rangers supporters are mostly Protestants. Emotions run high between these two clubs and their rivalry often reaches fever-pitch. The rivalry between the two Manchester clubs (City and United) is enormous, but the division between the two clubs does not normally result in the violent behavior exhibited by the Glasgow Celtic and Rangers fans.

It may be time for the US to see such rivalry by having more than one team at the highest level in the larger cities. It might be stirring up a hornet's nest of controversy by using this statement, but as long as someone out there takes the challenge of building more professional soccer clubs for the USA then it will be worth it.

For Business

There are cycles within the business life of a company or a group of companies.

– Start, Grow, Build, Decline, End

Every business has a start. It may be one person who takes up the challenge to fill a need in the marketplace. It doesn't matter whether it is a store; a service; or a product to be manufactured; the entrepreneur sees a gap which can be filled using current technology.

You will find there is normally a period of growth. The product may have a limited appeal, national or international appeal. For example, someone who produces and sells baseball caps with logos from the New York area may find a suitable ready market in New York City and New York State, but the market can becomes limited to those with a special link to New York or a hope to visit the place "one day." However, there is a company called Lids who produces baseball caps in a number of colors and then adds the logo of a city, sports team, or a humorous logo in the shop at the time of purchase. Lids are able to sell their products far and wide in the US and even abroad. The basis is the same but the options in Lids give a wider appeal to the product.

Building a company is the exciting phase where a large number of managers get busy to grow different aspects of the business. In previous years this would often have been accomplished by borrowing money from banks. Today, many banks are reluctant to lend any money until they have escaped from their current financial problems. Building a company when there are financial restrictions requires very careful

budgeting and managers will be held
responsible for any lapses of budgetary control.

Once the entrepreneurial spirit of the company
has diminished, there will be a period of
consolidation. Often this happens when the
original business owner, or director, ceases to
have direct control over the running of the
company. This results in the management
being performed by accountants. Accountants
have their place, but once they are in charge of
a company their impulse is to continue with a
very careful budgetary control, within the
working of the company. They are often
characterized by a lack of entrepreneurial
spirit. There is no reason to risk money on a
new product or location, which means the
business gradually, declines due to lack of
expansion of revenue from new projects and
products.

Once a company has begun to slide downhill

with an accountant in charge there is very little hope for a company. The accountant will cut expenditure to the bone and will try and ensure the company stays solvent. But in the end it will fail as there is no allowance for new entrepreneurial efforts to expand the product range. A failing company will find both managers and employees who have realized what is happening and will abandon their employment and seek jobs elsewhere. It is not a pretty picture but will accelerate the decline of the company due to the loss of experience in the management of the company and loss of confidence of the workforce.

One example of the problems of companies is the story of F.W. Woolworth in the UK. Woolworths (or Woolies as the British people knew it) started off in Pennsylvania. Some of the representatives from the parent company landed in the UK in 1909 and started the company. Over the years the company had good turnover and profits but back in the 1990's they began to look sad and sorry compared too many other high-street stores. They contracted and there was no attempt to change the company's presence, and the result was they closed in November 2008. There are some bright spots, and one branch has been reopened as Wellworth's. The name will keep going as an online store www.woolworths.co.uk but at present this is a blog and not offering anything for sale.

- Annual

For many of the team managers who are working today, they did not see the initial setup of the company, and will not be working for the company in their current role when the company finally winds up. However, everyone needs to be reviewed on a regular basis. Some of us see this as an enormous waste of time, as to do this review properly, will take both a manager's and the team member's time. What are we reviewing? We are reviewing the last year. It is time to look at the work which the individual has completed during the last year, and also how they performed. The review should also cover what the team members need in terms of training, and what would be the future role, or roles which they would be expected to perform.

Every existing organization (be it a with-profit or non-profit) will have procedures to perform an annual review of all the staff in the organization. Obviously in the case of a non-profit organization, it will be difficult to effectively review volunteers but there may be the need to offer training for some of these volunteers to offer them full-time paid jobs.

Another review which should be carried out each year is a review of the team workload to understand the changes which are occurring to the workload over the last year and project any changes for the next year. Any requests for extra staff or reductions in the number of staff in the team should then naturally arise out of the annual workload review.

For the manager of a soccer team the review at the end of the soccer season is essential. He must review of all the team members, and their current physical condition. Are there any injuries which need surgery or treatment now? Are there injuries or conditions which could be treated now rather than letting them flare up during the next season?

The statistics of the club's performance compared with the performance in the previous season, and the averages over the previous 5 seasons may be of interest to the supporters, but this will also expose the manager's strengths and weaknesses as well as the strength's and weaknesses of the various parts of the team.

Decisions will need to be made about players who can be sold and the positions where the team needs to be strengthened. The manager should always be looked to build and not simply to throw away the old team and replace.

Most teams would not have the finance to completely replace their team each year. Each manager, even the one's who have finished at the top of their league for the last 5 years, and those who have won tournaments must consider the members of the team who have caused them problems over the last season and the five seasons before.

In one sense being at the top of your game means your opposition will attempt to stop you during the next season. You must be ready to give them something new to face and not only the players and tactics you have used successfully this season.

Opportunities will abound as you face the realities of the last season's games and the prospect of the new season's opponents.

Chapter 9 Building Your Team

Building your team is a team effort and includes more than your team members and yourself. The effort is concentrated on you to bring people to the best place possible, in terms of their careers in your organization. You should realize the better you make people perform the more attractive they can become to being head-hunted. This can be from within your own organization as well as by a competitor or even an organization in another niche or environment. It is your best team members who may be poached by another team in your organization or may even leave the organization for another job.

Have A Long-Term Team Goals

As team manager do you understand what the goals are for the organization in the long term and the short term? In soccer the goals are easily defined. We are to get the best results, the best position in the league and the best revenue in terms of tickets, promotional sales and the players promoting sports wear and other gear.

Discuss With Your Manager/Owner/Board

For the manager in business, the general goals of the business is to sell more, paying less for it and be the best in your niche are obvious.

What are the specifics? Are there specific changes to production (where in the world or by what process) how will it affect your team and the skills they need? Let me give an example. If the plan is to open a new factory in India or China will any of the team need to be able to speak Mandarin (in Hong Kong Cantonese) or Hindi? Will these languages be enough to communicate or will another language be necessary? Will it be necessary to have some elements of flexible working, ensuring contacts can be made across the different time zones?

Will travel to these countries be necessary with the appropriate cultural awareness training? It is no good traveling to another country only to make a cultural error which will cause bad feelings for years to come. This is only one example but change is here to stay in terms of the location of factories and the processes of manufacturing. The details off how this will affect your team must be examined.

Follow Through With Staff

As soon as it is possible, tell your team about any changes. Keep them aware of what is going on and why. There is nothing worse for a team member to hear the rumor machine in an organization trying to process what is happening, getting it wrong and the team thinking you are to blame by keeping things from them. Inform the team about the changes, preferably when they are all together. There is nothing worse than people asking questions of you individually, and then the answers being badly communicated to other members of the team. Once everyone has the opportunity to get the questions answered and everyone hears the answers your leadership will grow.

Sometimes you have to get the team together and admit change is coming but you cannot say what the changes are until an official announcement is made. If you can tell everyone when the change will happen, it helps but again this isn't always possible.

Even If You May Not Be The One Who Will See The Goal Complete

This will vary from organization to organization. Sometimes there are rules about moving a team manager from one area of the business to another in order to progress the manager's experience. This was definitely the case in the UK Civil service some years ago. I do not know about within the US Federal and state administration.

You will see a plan being passed down for you, to start to plan, and train your team for the task ahead. The plan may cover a number of aspects in terms of training people and changing the team's work patterns. This may all take time. If someone needs to learn Mandarin or Cantonese it will be many years before they are completely fluent.

There are many issues of culture and attitude which also affect the communication of Chinese. When it comes to communicating with mainland Chinese (from the People's Republic of China) in English it is very hard to get them to accept they speak and write English well. Why this battle? The problem is the Chinese people for hundreds of years have been told, "They are too stupid to learn the Latin alphabet," (the basis of English) and they accept it as a matter of fact.

The opposite is the case. In order to learn written Chinese, you need to learn an enormous amount. For example, to read a Chinese newspaper requires you to know about 10,000 characters. Speaking in Chinese can get you into all sorts of problems. You could say Mei Ma in Chinese and it could be understood as "Buying a horse" if you use one tone and you wanting to "Selling your mother" in another tone.

Learning a language and also to understand the culture may take someone a very long time. The aim of communicating in a different language may start when you have accepted another post within your organization.

Build

When you want to build a building then you start by leveling what is there and digging foundations. With people, you must start where they are and build on their knowledge, experience, wisdom (or lack of it), and technical know-how. It is very tempting to start with a clean sheet and get rid of the existing team and start with your own team. This provides some challenges.

For the soccer team you may not have the finance to start from scratch and the fans, which are already attached to at least some of the members of the existing squad, will begin to object. If the fans reaction results in lower sales of tickets then you have made a really big mistake from which it is very difficult to recover. For the team in business, the knowledge of already doing the daily tasks of the team is held by the team members. It is sometimes not easy to see the little jobs which are being done with no fuss and yet they will keep the work flowing. It doesn't matter if it is getting more paper for the printer, or filling the coffee maker with water, every little job done without fuss makes the team more effective.

Sometimes you only notice those little jobs when someone is not at work.

We should build upon people's strengths and seek to minimize their weaknesses. There is a danger here, when we can make the team so efficient at performing its day-to-day tasks, and we no longer need everyone in the team and the result is being asked to cut team members.

Beware of the temptation to build your own empire. Most of us have seen it, the team leader who is mainly concerned with building their own empire. It doesn't matter if the plans of the team leader do not fully integrate with the company plans. The team of the empire builder must be the biggest, with the best people, the best equipment (especially computers), and occupy the most prominent position in the office. Whilst it may be tempting for the office to get these prestigious places the final result will be people noticing the excess and the person who caused it. We must always be a team player in the organization as a whole, not building our own empire.

Recruit New Team Members

The obvious way is either to advertise internally or externally for a vacancy. Today a third option is often used to simply hire a temporary worker to fill the gap. If they prove themselves to be good, you can offer them a permanent job, if they are not good, you can let them go and try someone else. The temporary job becomes an extended job interview. The advantage is a decision can be made over a period of time. If a person can perform their job adequately and fit in with the existing team members then they are offered a job. You should choose your recruitment techniques to solve your team needs.

As far as soccer is concerned there are many players available on free loan who have different styles and attitudes which can also be evaluated. In the end the really good players must be enticed to come and be part of your team. This may mean more money as well as a home, car, schools for any children, and security personnel. Are they worth it? This is for every club to decide.

When David Beckham signed up to play for L.A. Galaxy the name was instantly recognizable and the price tag of $250 million dollars for a 5 year contract, which gives about $1million a week in terms of salary and commercial endorsements. Maybe more European players could be persuaded to come to the US in order to build up the challenge of competing in the US soccer league.

Alter The Balance

What is the balance of your business team? Are they male/female; sexual orientation; married/ single/living together; or young/old. What are their outlooks on work? Are they all risk takers, or do they stick to the tried and tested methods built up over time? We have looked at this in Chapter 3 (Team analysis). The bottom line is what you think needs to be changed in order for the team to function better?

This may be impossible to decide, yet by bringing in a person with the same features and characteristics as the rest of the team may result in more conflict as the new person jockeys for "position" within the team. It may be easier to bring in someone who is the exact opposite of those who are there already there to change the balance. It might mean you bring in an older person among a group of workers in their 20's, and they see the work ethic which has been effective in the older person's life.

When you bring in a young person for a team who are older, and set in their ways can spark the enthusiasm which is currently missing from these older workers. Bringing in someone who has been married for a long time can challenge those who have a history of failed marriages and relationships; it may even bring some stability into their lives.

In the end you may decide the balance is right and try and keep with the status quo. Remember the decision is yours in the end.

Train And Develop The Individual

What do you think of each member of your team? There are some who are ripe for training courses (external or internal), special projects, or more responsibilities. Your role as team manager must be to stretch the individual until they can really begin to see their own potential. You should remember from time to time you will give your team member a task which is beyond their capabilities, and they will make mistakes. As team leader you will need to pick up the pieces, and the mess they are in, and take the time to rebuild their confidence. The buck stops with you when it comes to motivating and keeping your team members going.

When we consider the current world economic slowdown, training budgets may be cut, but it is essential to be developing the members of your team and getting your team on the courses they need.

Train Yourself

When you think of training it is essential to keep in mind your own training needs. Over and over again you will need to seek out your manager to make sure you are stretched and challenged. You will need to agree a training schedule for the year at your annual review, and try to make sure your boss sticks to it. In business things change, but training yourself is still important, and you need to make progress in the organization's salary scales and promotional structure. This may sound selfish, but unless you are progressing yourself you will find it difficult to help others to progress.

Train Your Successor

This is dealt with as a separate chapter (Chapter 12). We are including this note here to make sure you realize the complete picture and you realize there is one extra part which needs looking into.

Chapter 10 Painful Tasks

From time to time life and the organization (football club, company or non-profit) will leave the team manager with a hard job to do. It doesn't matter if you have never fired someone before, or if you have had to fire hundreds, it is hard. If you are dealing with someone of the opposite sex then make sure you have a chaperon to make sure you cannot be accused of anything improper.

Losing Staff

It is not often said, but the staff is the most important asset to any team. The effective blending of a number of individuals together to make an effective team will always have ups and downs, but it will always accomplish more to work as a team than to try and work as isolated individuals.

Do It Right

The first rule when you are facing uncertain times on the organization is to keep people informed. It helps to get people focused to do their jobs and not focus on the latest gossip. Yes, I know the person who cleans the executive toilets often knows what is happening before the managers, but sometimes they get it totally utterly and completely wrong.

The second rule is to deal with people as people. They are not slaves to be thrown a check, and a pink slip and be got rid of. People want some sort of reassurance, they need to know it was not their fault even when they know the organization is in trouble financially, they will always hope it will not be them who will end up losing their job.

The third rule is to make sure the person losing their job is talked to and has every opportunity to ask questions before they meet their colleagues. There is nothing worse for the person who is leaving, going out and really giving vent to their anger in front of the rest of the team, but behind your back.

The fourth rule is to communicate the facts of who is losing their jobs and when to the whole of the team. Sometimes it is necessary for the person losing their job to complete a period of project work before they can be released.

Follow Up 1-To-1 With People Who Are Left Behind And Their Concerns

The greatest danger when someone is fired or made redundant is for the resulting insecurity which persuades the other team members to search for new employment.

Once the individual or individuals leave their chosen employment to join the ranks of the unemployed, it is time to have a heart to heart with all of the remaining team members. As we said under "Do it right" we must keep people informed. You should stress you have kept them informed at every stage where you were allowed to inform them. There is no way around this. When you keep people informed they see the daylight. If you do not inform them they feel like mushrooms. (note Mushrooms are kept in the dark, once in a while someone opens the door and lets in a little light then they are covered with manure – this in industry is sometimes called the "Mushroom syndrome")

Now the ax has fallen, it's been months of conjecture, and the time has come to reassure the people. A person worked part-time for a charity, and when he informed the other leaders in the charity, he was about to be made redundant, they all said he was imagining things.

What these men failed to take into account was the fact the local company he was working for had been taken over by one of its big competitors. The working practices were very different in the new management. It was not until the day the redundancies were announced, and the person told the other leaders, and they realized he was right.

The shock hits home to those who are left. Computer passwords have to be changed, and the next few months will be characterized by the few trying to cover the work of the many. The whole attitude of the team can change from one of working together "happily" to one of fear and doubt over who will be next to lose their job.

You need to talk to everyone left on the team. Reassure them their jobs are now more secure than they were before.

Finally, encourage all of your remaining staff to come and talk with you if they have any concerns for their job security, or if they hear any rumors.

Saving Money

What do you do when you get an instruction from your manager when you have to cut the costs of your department? There are two ways to approach it for the team manager either secrecy or openness.

The secrecy approach means, you know where there will need to be cuts made in the overheads, and you know the money must come from your budget. You look at the team and its expenses and try to work out a way of cutting the costs which would leave most of your team intact, and yet save money. This is hard work.

The other option is openness. Simply, you tell your team, there is a need to cut costs and we need some innovative solutions to save money.

You will work on this collectively. Some of the options which team members have come up with are shown below. One thing to remember is for you as a manager and all the other managers, it is not very prudent to expect cuts in overheads, and then go away on an all-expenses-paid business trip soon after the exercise. Let's all be sensitive to those around us who are hurting due to shortage of finance.

Cuts In Salary And Benefits Rather Than Lose Job

Some workers would far rather earn less and keep the jobs they have. They may have faced periods of unemployment before and not be willing to fight their way through the hard times again. This approach may be easier in a small company where all the employees can agree to take a pay cut rather than in a multi-national company where some will want to keep both job and existing salary.

Renegotiate Leasing

We live in times when landlords are finding it harder and harder to get tenants, if you do not own your own premises then renegotiate the lease. If you own your own premises then it may be possible to renegotiate the taxes you are paying on the property in order to keep everyone employed.

Cut Out Free Coffee/Tea Or Doughnuts

You will find a lot of people are dieting, or they will they be discussing how to change their eating habits. If you do not have as much money as you once had, your diet will change; you will be looking for cheaper cuts of meat and less of it, cheaper vegetables, potatoes, rice, pasta and bread. Also, it will be a time where people will look completely at their eating habits, and possibly make a move to a more healthy diet. It might be when you charge a nominal price for the cost of a coffee; you will increase your revenue and you will change this from a liability to an asset. Let's be clear there is a cost to provide free drinks and cakes. Cease to pay for it and the costs disappear and you may even begin to make money on the deal. Also, people will stop and think about their eating and drinking habits at work. You will find a lot less coffee is being used, because people are no filling their cup, and not drinking it, and when it has gone cold, throwing it away, and getting a refill.

When you ask for help from your team members, you'll begin to tap into the energy and imagination of the team members. You should also take a note of those with the best ideas as you may need their input again on new projects when the economy picks up.

Stop A Project

This is a hard one to tackle. Your pet project is going well, in a few months it will begin to provide revenue to the company and pay back the company handsomely for its efforts. But the accountants have decided it is time to cut the project and not to continue with it.

It may be you can make a request for the company to keep the project open, and you'll work one evening a week unpaid on the project to complete the work which is needed. It may work or you may see all your hard work thrown away by someone who is only looking at what has been spent, and not at the potential return. In the end you have to let the project go if it is your manager's decision. Sometimes, decisions are made by those who understand nothing about the benefits, but only see the costs which have already been incurred. It can be one of the hardest things to face as a manager, and disappointing for the team who have worked so hard on the project.

Chapter 11 Quietness And Confidence

It is essential for your team to know how you will react to them and the problems they face. To manage will also mean to cope with crises. Sometimes, these crises are the result of mistakes by your team, other times they are mistakes from others, but the reality is, "The buck stops with you" when you became the manager of the team. One American president used to have on his desk the reminder "The Buck Stops Here." We must often look into the problems handed to us as tests for our next promotion, or a way for senior management to hasten our exit from the company.

Extreme Circumstances

From time to time every team faces extreme circumstances. Few can be as extreme as British Airways flight 5390 on June 10th 1990. The flight-plan was a simple fly from

Birmingham International Airport in the UK, to
Malaga Airport in a BAC-111.

The aircraft was still climbing when one of the
aircraft's front windshields flew off in an
explosive decompression. The captain was
sucked out and only held inside the plane by
one of the stewards. The details are shown on
National Geographic's Air Crash Investigation
programs.

The teamwork between the 1st officer, cabin
crew, and ground controllers meant the
captain's life was saved and everyone landed
safely at Southampton Airport. Your team may
never face such life-and-death moments, but
we all face trying times in business and in sport
when our character and the character of our
team is put to the most severe test.

Tsunami

Many of us remember the pictures on our televisions on December 26th, 2004 when a tsunami hit many countries in Asia. How did team work help people survive this terrible event? Very simply, they worked together as a team, to get out of the disaster area and to a place of safety. Talking to people in one camp, we found a lady in her 70's who was proud of the way she had avoided the wave, and arrived at a safe place. Her escape was on the back of a motorbike. Now, you might think there is nothing strange about that, but, the motorbike had 7 people on it, all who arrived at a safe place. They lost everything they owned, but they had their lives, and a motorbike to get out of the camp.

They continued to work as a team, as the government put people from the same villages into one camp. Many camps didn't work as teams, and they faced more difficulties than was necessary. For many people, it was about self, they grabbed whatever they could get, without regard to the other people around.

But, this group worked as a team. They made the decision, anything they received they would store until they had enough to give to everybody. This way, there was no arguing about someone having more than another person. It was equal sharing. Mattresses and pillows were stored as we had to keep returning to the stores to buy more for them, and our restriction was only because of what our vehicles could carry.

They told us about the need for the children to have fresh fruit, and it was simple to go out in our vehicle, and find someone who had fruit to sell. We bought a truckload for a few dollars, and took it back to the camp. There was no rushing, because they worked as a team, and stood in an orderly queue waiting to get their share.

The leaders of the village were concerned for the children, they had no toys or games, and got bored walking aimlessly around the camp on weekends. Again, for us with a vehicle it was simple to go and buy some soccer balls, badminton sets and coloring books. Yes, it was simple but the kids immediately took the soccer balls, and soccer teams were all around the camp. It was great to see even the youngest of the children getting involved, and nobody telling them they were not able to play because they didn't know the rules.

Disasters do happen, but it really does depend on the team members how they decide to work together.

No Anger

Some bosses say quietly "Shit Happens" and

the bottom line is, something will go wrong, even when it shouldn't and the likelihood of it happening is a million-to-one. Unfortunately, with computerized systems and large databases these possibilities turn up far more often than we would like.

It is easy to get angry when you are in trouble, especially when you didn't cause it, and you didn't see it coming. Do not take your anger out on your staff? This will only make them edgy and will cause them to move from your team (either within your organization or outside of it) and then the problems only get worse as you have lost both experience and expertise which you'll need.

This may be very difficult for the soccer team manager. There have been times when a refereeing decision has gone against his team, and the manager temper boils over. It is especially true when one of his team is badly injured, or sent off. It is not unknown for the manager to be sent from the touchline to the stands to cool off. In some rare instances the Football Association will ban the manager from the dugout for a period and send him or her to sit in the stands.

No Tantrums

You should be looking for no emotional outbursts of bad temper, no tirades where you run down the person or organization who has put you into this problem. If you break out like this then your team will never know when this may come in their direction. They will regard you like a firework which is about to explode at any moment. Communication from your team to you will be cut to the absolute minimum as they do now know how you will react.

Monthly Cycles

Women and men have differences. With some female team members, you can trace their monthly cycles by watching their moods exhibited in different parts of the month (28 days).

This directly affects the female manager as she must be aware if she suffers mood swings during the month. She must consider when it happens in the monthly cycle and take medical advice to find appropriate ways of controlling these mood swings. The control may mean relaxation and stress classes or medication.

This also affects the management of women, because she may react completely differently in one part of her cycle to another. There are no hard-and-fast rules on this as every woman is different and some exhibit no negative attitudes at all.

One final thing to realize is women can have babies. If a woman starts acting out of character then make a note of it, as this may be the first sign of a baby on the way. It will vary from country to country, when a woman will stop work in order to have the baby. It also varies when and if she will return to work. Once she makes it official and tells people she is pregnant, and then makes sure you are fully aware of the company and legal requirements of dealing with a pregnant member of staff. There are requirements of pre-natal checks with the doctor

Do not assume a woman's monthly cycles only affect the woman herself. It may be you have a man on your team who is upset and jumpy at certain times of the monthly cycle. It may not be because the man has a cycle, but his girlfriend; partner; wife; flat mate; or landlady has really bad attitudes at this time of the month and it affects everybody they come in contact with. This may not be the time to approach the problem directly but if it gets too bad then a quiet talk with them may help reassure them it is the monthly cycle which affects some women more than others.

Quiet Demeanor In Any Crisis

In the office this is essential. The UK's Commercial Union (Insurance Company) slogan was "We won't make a drama out of a crisis" should be the aim of any manager. What has happened? Is it the computer failure which has caused you to lose millions of records and means the computer system will be unavailable for days or weeks?

You might have had a break in, where the company records and petty cash have been stolen.

Even worse you have the death of a key member of staff in an accident or through an illness.

These entire problems can throw the team or

even the whole company into a panic. The manager needs to quietly assess the situation, come up with strategies to keep the team functioning, and be ready to deal with senior managers, and keep them informed.

It is easy to set up the "fight or flight" reaction, but the team manager needs to keep it all together for the benefit of his team and the company as a whole. It may be as you review what has happened in this crisis, you realize how you need more training in the aspect of dealing with crises. Always remember, a crisis can occur at any time. Usually it will seem to occur at the worst time. Your team will see the way you handle yourself in a crisis and learn from you.

On the sports field (soccer; football; baseball; basketball etc) it's not easy. The person who stands out with his catchphrase of "You cannot be serious" is John McEnroe. Whenever something went really bad on the tennis court in the match he was playing he used it. His temper on the court was legendary but off the court, he kept it under control. The same can be true of some players in soccer. Eric Cantona of Manchester United in January 1995 attacked a fan kicking him, and trading punches with him after being sent off. The adrenaline was running high, and the error was made on the pitch which resulted in the Frenchman being sent off.

His reaction to the fan then resulted in the police becoming involved. Managers get into the same predicament. In 2001 Lawrie Sanchez was fined £2,000 and banned from the touchline for 3 matches after an incident at the Wycombe Wanderers vs. Leicester City FA Cup match where he vented his frustration on the linesman after Wycombe were refused a penalty.

The final example is from a manager who needs no introductions, the Manchester United manager Sir Alex Ferguson. He was banned from the touchline and fined after using insulting words to the match referee at half-time in Bolton's defeat of Manchester United by 1-0. All of us can let our anger get the better of us but it gains nothing.

Confidence In Your Own Authority

It doesn't matter if it is delegated authority, be confident in it. One of the greatest problems in the Western World today is the matter of authority. Who has it; who can use it; who can refuse it? The president of the USA has the authority over the United States. This has checks and balances, which has been brought into the system by the senators and representatives of the States of the Union. However, when it comes to another country the president of the United States is seen as someone with enormous power in terms of military and financial might, but with no authority to order, only a responsibility to persuade. There are always limits to authority.

Talking to a people I realize, fifty years ago there was no argument as to who had the authority in the home, it was the father. No wonder there was a TV program some time ago with the title "Wait, 'til your father gets home!" Over the last half a century the authority in the home has shifted. With so many absent fathers (both physically and emotionally); control in the home now lies in the hands of the children. When the child leaves home either to go to college or to start work, they face the conflict with authority. If the child now faces the authority of the military or an older person they may come into line with authority, but if the person is a similar age then there could easily be a battle for the dominant role even though the team manager is the one with authority. In the worst case scenario the new team member may need to be dismissed from the team (both in terms of soccer and in business).

You will find as the team manager you need to be confident of his or her own authority. There shouldn't be any debate in your mind what you control, and what you do not. In the end most authority is delegated, but the knowledge of how much authority the manager has and the way the manager exerts their authority. You will soon see how hard it is to control someone who cannot accept authority.

Beware Of Humor

What is your humor like? Are you appreciated for your humor by your friends and family, or is this something they would rather you avoided using? It may seem very simple statement, but humor from a manager can backfire.

It can be misunderstood. It can be unhelpful. It can create confusion especially when in a multi-cultural environment. Even with people from your own state a misunderstanding caused by a humorous remark can take a long time to repair.

What can be done?

Firstly, avoid unnecessary humor especially if it is at the expense of someone else on the team. Beware of making humorous remarks about someone on another team. It may be a soccer manager, in making a humorous remark about a player from another team will make his own team members wary about what jokes he makes about them.

Secondly, always be thinking about the humor which your team members use between each other. Make sure they know what you think if funny and what may be taking things too far. Do not make it a heavy thing but make people aware how humor can hurt the person it is aimed at. The team is bigger than one individual and must stay together without hurtful humor aimed solely at one team member. This comment is even truer when the humor is aimed at someone who has suffered an injury. Many injuries in soccer are not the fault of the person who is injured, and can lead to the end of a career.

Thirdly, keep your humor within the limits you prescribe for your team members. When they talk to you they need to know you take their fears and concerns seriously, even when they have nothing to worry about.

Fourthly, make sure you have made it very clear when you are being funny, and are not being serious.

Finally, while it is true, a little bit of light relief does help in pressurized situations on the soccer pitch or in the office environment,

misunderstandings can ruin the team spirit
and sap everyone's strength in trying to repair
the damage.

Chapter 12 Train Your Successor

One of your major tasks is to train someone to take your place. There is no way you can stay in charge of this team for ever. Yes, you may be coming up to retirement, and may want to stay where you are until the final day of work, however, the company will still want you to be training the next team leader. The deputy team leader may have just been promoted, and you will have to start all over again.

Examine Your Team

Start with the group of people you have. Look at them and see who has the potential for leadership. There are too many who want promotion but they are not really team leaders or team managers. You can decide who are the potential leaders, and seek to get them to receive sufficient training to lead a team. After the training the team manager needs to evaluate the report from the trainer or trainers to see if your evaluation of the person's abilities is echoed by the trainers.

Choose Your Deputy

Once you find the best, you will need to get them to act as your deputy. There will always be the need for you to have a deputy. Holidays will always be part of the year and you need your time off as much, or sometimes more than the people on the team you manage. Why not take the opportunity of seeing how your deputy manager performs in your holiday period?

Ensure Proper Training And Resources.

Once you know who your deputy and replacement will be, your organization's training syllabus comes into play and all the right training needs to be given and any examinations or tests completed and passed. There are many times when there seem to be too many hoops to jump through, but many organizations know the dangers of promoting someone into a team manager's role too soon. You should find out what is necessary and what is recommended.

Look at the resources in terms of books (including this one), videos and even role-playing games to be immediately available for their use.

Chapter 13 Communication

Do you think communication is difficult? Have you found there are often people who talk a great deal, but do not communicate a single simple piece of real information about the company or where the company is going?

A person, who worked on contract in commercial IT for many years, told me in almost every company he worked under contract "The left hand doesn't know what the right hand is doing." Over and over again in companies large and small the communication of what was going on with all these IT specialists in the company "doing something" was not communicated even to the people they were supporting or developing systems for.

It is vital for the team to know where they are going, and what they are doing and what is still to be done. Sometimes the orientation of new employees needs to include where the company has come from, how it started and how it was given its name.

One final thing about communication and it is obvious as soon as you look at someone is you should "Listen twice as much as you speak." If a team member comes to you with a problem or a task which needs some decisions always have the decency to either ask for a "time out" as you are about to go for another meeting and make an appointment to meet up, or hear them out there and then. The team needs to know they have your ear and your attention.

History

The team should know what the history of the company is, and how they grew. Take as an example Hewlett Packard. Now it is an enormous manufacturer of computers and printers. It started in a garage (not one like you have at home but a commercial garage where cars are repaired). The decision was made by Mr. Hewlett and Mr. Packard for them to join together and make the best electrical measurement equipment in the world. They still do, but this is not the reason they are well known by the majority of the public. The general public makes the connection with their name because of their knowledge of computers. People who make, test and repair electrical equipment make contact with their excellent test equipment.

The same for a soccer club. When did it start? Where was the first ground? What was the first trophy? Who are in the hall of fame of the best players? The current generation should know all this without even having to think about it.

Current Events

Change is here to stay. Any business, organization, or even a soccer club. Anyone who stands still, will not progress. Every business is looking to increase ROI (Return on Investment). Every non-profit is looking to extend its reach and the number of people who they are helping. Every soccer club wants to extend its unbeaten record, to win the league and the national and international tournaments. Every player wants to represent his or her country an international level.

It is your job to keep everyone informed, and this will include those people who clean the toilets, to the board level directors. From the man who cuts the grass and cleans out the stands to the owner of the football club. Tell them what is going on.

Future Plans

The computer laser printer had a very shaky start. When the original ones were built they were installed on mainframe computers to print enormous volumes of output. The paper was fed into the printer in drums which were too heavy to be lifted by one person, which meant mechanical devices had to be used. When they started printing one of the computer operators had to be standing by with a fire extinguisher to use if the paper caught on fire. When Hewlett Packard entered the LaserJet market with the LaserJet 1 it was revolutionary. Here was a printer able to print hundreds of pages of A4 or letter size paper. It was far quieter than the dot-matrix printers which had dominated the personal computer market until then. Today, laser and inkjet printers are in every office and very many homes. Color lasers are now available. All because HP started to produce the LaserJet 1.

As with any other company and soccer team the changes which are coming need to be communicated. If the soccer team is going to be rebuilt due to some basic problems with the team, and the need to start again, then the team needs to know what the changes are and how those changes will affect them.

Pep Talk

The soccer team manager knows he or she has to talk to, and motivate the players. This is as essential in the half-time break, as it is before the start of the match. There may be other times when a manager will give the team a pep talk. It goes with the soccer manager's job and is an expected part of every match and season and cup campaign.

For the manager in a business or non-profit it is not a clear-cut. When do I give a pep talk? For some managers where there are seasonal pressures in the production, and work process, it is obvious we need to encourage people beforehand. For example in the food industry there may be specific periods when production and orders need to be high.

For example at Thanksgiving, Christmas, and

Easter where high volumes of food like whole turkeys are consumed. It could be at Ramadan, if you are preparing food for the Muslims (they do feast after sunset in their fasting period). Everything needs to be in place. Some workers will be starting early, and finishing late in order to make sure everything is available at the right time in the right place, and is a fresh as possible. Nothing is left to chance. Before the season starts the manager will encourage his workers to perform even better than they did last year. At the end of the busy period there will be time for a rest.

So communicate; communicate; and communicate.

Chapter 14 Different Organizational Stresses And Strains

Different organizational models mean different stresses on the team leader and his teams. I am deliberately looking at business models here and not soccer teams.

A Private Limited Company, Partnership Or Sole Trader

Here we have a person or a group of people in control. They control the destiny and direction of the company. There may be loans which are outstanding, and bills to be paid, but the business owner will be aware of them and make provisions for them in his business plan. The pressures are simple to please the person who is in charge. If the ownership of the company changes, then the requirements of the new owner will be different but a transfer of power takes time and everyone will need to adjust.

A Public Limited Company

Here I am talking about a company which has
shares traded on the stock market. It doesn't
matter if the stock market is NYSE; London or
Hong Kong, the same pressures come. The
board is in charge, they have to be followed and
obeyed.

However, the shareholders have a vested
interest in two things. They have a vested
interest in seeing the value of their shares grow,
and in seeing dividends being paid out. For too
many shareholders, the operation of the
company on a day-to-day basis is immaterial.
The shareholders concern is what they see on
the stock market. They want the share price
going up, even if the shares of everyone else in
a particular industry are going down. Although
the board of directors and ultimately the CEO
(chairman of the board or whatever title they
take) runs the company, he or she will always
have their eyes on the share price and the

reaction of shareholders to any changes they make.

A Non-Profit

This could be a charitable organization or a religious foundation (church, denomination, mosque, synagogue or monastery). The basic bottom line for the non-profit organization is to get their contributors contributing and not only keep them giving but also encouraging others to give. They must keep their running costs as low as possible. This can vary markedly between urban and rural settings. A church in a rural location may not be able to pay their minister a large salary, but church members may very well give fruit and vegetables to supplement the minister's stipend. In an urban setting the salary may be larger, but the expenses of buying and keeping a large premises, and a large number of support workers for the church may be enormous.

The costs element is especially relevant for the charitable organization. Today there are more and more urban poor in the world (including North America). The problem is getting worse as people lose their livelihood and their homes all across the world in the current recession. There is no easy answer, except the support of charities. Some people would rather die than take charity, but it is not as easy as that.

The non-profit must communicate well with its supporters and make sure they are aware of what the non-profit is accomplishing, and what their needs are. The last thing which the non-profit wants to do is to have is a bad reputation in the media. If donor finance dries up then any charitable work stops, permanent employees lose their livelihood and eventually the whole charity stops and fails.

A Volunteer Team

For completeness I am including managing a volunteer team. Some of you will find yourselves in charge of a volunteer team to perform some task. It could be the search for a missing child, or a clearing up of some forestry which has become overgrown or full of rubbish.

A group of volunteers are very different from a team of employees. The only thing holding the team together is their desire to perform a task, or simply to help. They need to be persuaded, far more than being ordered. You need a clear idea of the tasks which are priority and which are a secondary task. Finding a child alive is a priority, finding clothing or discarded items is a secondary task, but finding clothing may become a primary task if the child is found but is no longer alive. We may need to clear away rubbish and junk before the forest can be cleared. We have to persuade and encourage and then complete the job.

Consider what can be done before you start to accept the task. Make sure you know what the task is and you understand the task, and the team is able to be encouraged before you start the task.

Chapter 15 Distractions

Most managers find on a regular basis, there are tasks to do which takes them away from their team and their real work into an area where the whole of the business or the organization comes into focus. For the team manager there may be many major issues around the preparation of these tasks.

Budgets

Often we do not hear about this when we look at a soccer team, but no team has bottomless pockets. Not even Chelsea in the English Premier league has a completely open-ended cash fountain. There have to be agreements about what can be spent and a budget set up.

For a soccer team this can mean there is the possibility of losing players to bring in revenue, as well as gaining others. This is not a simple process, but too many players in any area of the field, and too little flexibility in their positions can mean losing a player. The supporters and the people may not like the changes which are being made. The changes may result is lost revenue in terms of ticket sales. All this must be looked into when it comes to making decisions about gaining or losing players. The manager of a soccer team must always consider whether he could be the next one to be axed to save money.

In a business setting this may not be the easiest thing to do. It could be simply the management needs to cut costs and your team is high on the list for cutting costs. It could be a way for good revenue is expected with the work being done by your team, and there will be the need to increase staff levels. This recession will not last forever so both scenarios will have to be faced. It is always best if the budget can be agreed, and no cutbacks are made during the financial year. Trying to cut costs during the latter part of a year can be very difficult and stressful for the manager. These scenarios need to be faced when they happen and working through them in detail is not helpful.

Staff Reporting Procedure

This is simple but, often forgotten by managers. Your manager will be preparing a report on you at the same time you are preparing a report on your team.

It may be the team you are manager of, or the business you are part of does not have a formalized staff reporting procedure. It is then the responsibility of the team manager to find a suitable mechanism to report on each team member.

The report will look at the strengths and weaknesses exposed during the previous twelve months (or soccer season if it is more appropriate). The report will review the relationships with other team members and any problems which have surfaced. The report will then go on to look at any new training which is required or new responsibilities which will cause the team member to grow in their current position and to set them free to grow into a team captain or manager role.

A review like this will often help the "rising stars" to realize there are continuing challenges which they will face. It can be seen as many new players will find a great deal of freedom in their first year in a particular league, and then the opposition defenses or forwards will learn to cope with them. The player will need to practice new skills, and develop new talents in order to continue to be a vital part of the team.

It is different in a business environment. We put someone to perform a task which is in his or her capabilities and then they can continue to perform the same job with no challenges and no promotion for years. The wise manager will not let this happen. The manager will examine the strengths and weaknesses of the team member and will seek to build them up to fill greater and greater responsibilities, with greater and greater rewards. Some people will not have any desire to move into management, especially when they are working in a technical capacity, a management role may move them away from what they are good at.

It will take time and effort to appraise the work of each individual of your team. Once the appraisal is completed then the training and developmental opportunities will need to be considered, especially in the light of the budget cutbacks.

In reality we are continually appraising our team, but once a year it is good to put it down in writing and review it with the team member in order to make progress with the individual and the team.

Your Project Work

As team leader there will be some pet project
which you are involved with. This may be
setting up a youth squad at the soccer team,
which will encourage local boys and girls to
enjoy soccer. It will need the budget to do it and
committed staff to build up the team and keep
the children enthusiastic.

Many clubs in Britain and Europe encourage
participation from a young age. These children
will be fans and will often want to play for the
team. This may not always be possible at first,
but the task of encouraging new talent into the
game of soccer is an ongoing process for all
clubs at all levels in all the continents.

In business there will be some work which
you'll want to keep to yourself. It may be
replacing the library of books which are

reference manuals for your business by having electronic copies of the same books and book readers. These readers may be Amazon's Kindle or Sony Reader. For a multi-national company it would probably have to be the Sony, as Kindle's cannot access the Internet outside of the USA. Here will be a project for you to perform, and once it has been evaluated the new books can be made available wherever they are needed.

Projects give the manager a piece of work to do which doesn't necessarily mean simply managing the team but contributing to the club or to the business area they manage.

Conclusion

We have looked at your team and your position as a team manager of a soccer team.

Where are you going as a team?
Are you going up or down in the soccer league?
Where will the team be in 12 months time?
Will you still be the manager?

The same situation is faced by the manager in a business. The prospects are less risky in business, but there are times when you are in the wrong place at the wrong time.

A team can function in the most extreme of circumstances. The example of the rescue teams who went into the Italian city of L'Aquila and its surrounding villages bears testimony of the results which many hundreds of people can accomplish.

They were expecting a quiet Easter and suddenly they were involved in the life and death struggle to rescue hundreds of people from their collapsed homes and apartments.

We are always acting on the normal run-of-the-mill tasks until one day something explodes on us. There is nothing we can do to anticipate this change, and our job is to dig the organization out of the trouble it has got into. Here we need extreme flexibility from everyone so we can get back on the rails.

As I bring this guide to a close I want to point you to one extreme frustration you will face. The frustration is the person "on" your team who refuses to take any team management responsibility. You may remember in the film "The Guns of Navarone" Gregory Peck has a wonderful line when driving home the necessity of leadership to David Niven. The line goes like this "You think you've been getting away with it all this time, standing by. Well son, You're by-standing days are over, you're in this now son, right up to your neck." This is obvious in the film which David Niven's character had to take responsibility for his actions, and take the lead in blowing up the guns.

We have to make sure our team shares the load in performing the tasks we are responsible for, and then we can complete our tasks. It doesn't matter if we are a soccer team manager who needs to put together a string of victories to avoid losing his job, or a business team manager who needs help to keep the business running for another month, and then another month until this recession is over. We all need to lead and encourage our teams to continue to perform over and above their abilities.

My final quote is a warning for all managers in soccer, sports or in the business world. It Comes from Michael Jordan who should know a great deal about winning championships. The quote is a telling one "Talent wins games, but teamwork and intelligence wins championships." You can build your team with the most talented individuals, yet they will not always win. Your team needs people of intelligence who will perform as part of the team, and not just when the spotlight is on them. Then your team will succeed in sports and in business in the long term.